A Harvest of
Healing Foods

A Harvest of Healing Foods

RECIPES AND REMEDIES FOR THE MIND, BODY, AND SOUL

CHRISTINE McFADDEN

CONSULTANT: KATHLEEN M. ZELMAN

WHITECAP BOOKS

CLB 4958

This edition published in 1998 by Whitecap Books Ltd.,
351 Lynn Avenue, North Vancouver, B.C., Canada V7J 2C4

Printed and bound in Singapore
ISBN 1-55110-649-3

Created by *Anthology*
Brighton, Sussex, England

FOR ANTHOLOGY:
Editorial and Design Direction: *Rhoda Nottridge*
Nutritional Consultant: *Kathleen M. Zelman*
Nutritional Analysis: *Pat Bacon*
Editor: *Jo Richardson*
Photography: *Don Last*, assisted by *Penny Hayler*
Home Economy: *Christine France*
Electronic Page Make-Up: *Ginny Zeal*
Index: *Dr. Caroline Eley*

FOR QUADRILLION:
Commissioning Editor: *Will Steeds*
Production: *Neil Randles, Karen Staff, Ruth Arthur*
Color reproduction: *Withers Litho, England*

Author's Acknowledgment
I would like to thank my husband and son for their unfailing love and support while writing this book. Sincere thanks also to Katy Balfry for her tireless recipe testing, to editor Jo Richardson for her patience and tact, to Rhoda Nottridge for giving me the opportunity to write about a subject dear to my heart, to Christine France and Don Last for the beautiful photography, and to nutritionist Kathleen Zelman for her invaluable advice.

Publisher's Note
The Publishers have made every attempt to ensure that all dietary information and advice, recipes, and other material contained in this book is accurate, and that it accords with current nutritional and medical practice as understood by the author and consultant nutritionist. However, the Publishers wish to state that none of the material contained herein is offered as medical advice, and warn readers that it should not be taken as such; in any case of doubt, consult your medical adviser. The Publishers also wish to advise readers that all information, advice, recipes, and other material contained in the book applies to adults, not children.

Contents

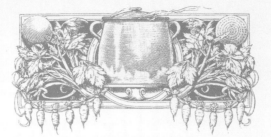

Introduction

Most of us would agree that optimum health is not merely the absence of disease but also involves a sense of well-being, of feeling full of energy and free from anxiety. However, the fast-moving and often stressful nature of life in the 1990s means that your state of health may fall short of this ideal. Although you may not be able to control fully certain aspects of your life which determine your state of health — environmental pollutants, financial insecurity, overwork, for instance — the one factor over which you have most control and which contributes directly to your state of health is what you eat.

Becoming more knowledgeable about the therapeutic properties of food and gradually making small but positive changes to what and how you eat can make an enormous difference to your physical, emotional, and spiritual being. The choices you make about foods reflect your attitude to yourself and to those you shop and cook for. They can also determine the fulfillment you get from life and the good you put into it.

A *Harvest of Healing Foods* explains all you need to know to take advantage of the therapeutic powers of foods. The book takes a holistic approach but is based on sound scientific principles. Instead of dwelling on "culprit" foods, it shows you how to think positively and get a feel for what might be good for you as an individual, and then to eat more of such foods, cooking them imaginatively and with enjoyment.

The introduction begins with an explanation of ancient healing practices, covering the concept of the vital life-force or *chi* — integral to most traditional practices, and shows how food has always played a part in the healing process. The introduction goes on to explain the historical background to nutritional science, and takes an impartial look at current nutritional claims. We look at what makes a healthy, balanced diet and compare this with healthy diets around the world. We also evaluate different diets currently used in the West. There is a brief discussion of the factors which influence our decisions on what to eat, and advice on how and when to eat in order to benefit fully from the nourishment that food has to offer.

The next section is divided into ten chapters of inspirational snacks and meals to take you through the day, beginning with "Gentle Awakenings" and ending with "Sunset Soothers". The recipes are bursting with flavor and color — and they are healthy. Some of them are a little time-consuming to prepare but the emphasis is on relaxation and enjoyment. In these days of fast food, let us not lose sight of the fact that cooking can be a pleasurable way of winding down at the end of a stressful day. It is also a way of saying "I love you," either to yourself, your partner, or your family.

The final section of the book begins with an explanation of individual nutrients and their function, and which foods contain them. Then follows an explanation of some common nutritional terms, and a section on health-promoting cookware and cooking methods. The major healing foods are then described in detail, followed by a nutritional analysis of each recipe. The book finishes with a list of useful addresses.

Nutritional claims

Throughout this book, foods are often described as being an "excellent", "rich," "good," or "useful" source, or just a "source" of a particular nutrient. These terms describe the nutritional value of a food in relation to the Recommended Dietary Allowance (RDA) recommended by the US Deparment of Agriculture. "Excellent" refers to foods which provide 100% of the RDA; "rich" means they supply 75%; "good" 50%; and "useful" 25%. A food that is said to be a 'source' of a nutrient contains at least 10% of the RDA.

TRADITIONAL HEALING AND HEALTHY EATING

Throughout history, food has been deeply rooted in our social, cultural, and spiritual lives, sometimes proving to be a stronger force among peoples than many other influences. Cultures throughout the world have long believed that the benefits from food go far beyond the sustenance simply provided by nutrients and calories. In ancient Greece, the Athenians believed that mealtimes were an opportunity to replenish the spirit as well as the body; they reclined on couches while eating and food was accompanied by music, poetry, and dancing. Shintoism, the national religion of Japan, treats the growing, preparation, serving, and eating of food as a sacred act. The Japanese have a saying "ishoku dogen" which means literally "medicine and food have the same source." This saying has been passed down from generation to generation for thousands of years and promotes the fact that without a daily intake of nourishing, wholesome food, health declines and physical and psychological symptoms inevitably appear. Our growing awareness of the link between what we eat and the effect it has on our physical, mental, and spiritual health acknowledges the thinking behind this ancient wisdom.

The life force

Most traditional healing methods are based on a belief in a dynamic life force, known in the East as *chi* or *prana* — the source of all growth and movement — flowing through acupuncture energy channels and maintaining the activity of body systems and organs. The presence or absence of *chi* in food, and the quality of the *chi* itself, is thought to influence all aspects of health and well-being. Food containing good *chi* will taste better and impart some of its life-force to the person who eats it. A person with dynamic, free-flowing *chi* will be bursting with vitality, with all body systems — particularly digestion and circulation — in perfect running order.

Eastern traditions

Based on the concept of *chi* and the principle of yin and yang, the Chinese system of healing is one of the most ancient and long-standing in the world, and has probably had more influence on modern holistic medicine in the West than any other healing tradition. The theory of yin and yang states that everything in the universe is interconnected. Within this whole, all phenomena are kept in balance and harmony by the opposition of two forces, which are either yin or yang in quality. The Chinese apply the concept to every single aspect of life. When applied to the diet, the yin and yang nature of our food is thought to have a great effect on our health and well-being. Yang foods are said to be warming, sweet, pungent, and energizing, whereas yin foods are cooling, salty, bitter, and sour, and help build blood and other bodily fluids. Eating too much of either type of food is thought to create an imbalance, resulting in ill health.

Another eastern healing tradition is the ancient Indian science of Ayurveda, meaning "science of life." Based on Vedic texts dating back over 4,000 years, Ayurvedic wisdom has been passed down through generations of Indian families and medical practitioners to become a widely used and long-standing method of healing which, like the Chinese tradition, has also been adopted in the West. Ayurveda teaches that food is divine and that the process of eating is one of the most intimate interactions between man and nature; the life or intelligence in food not only preserves each individual but becomes the individual; and that most disease is ultimately traceable to a poor diet. In Ayurveda, every taste and aspect of food has a specific effect on the physiology and psychology of the person eating it. Supported by meditation, yoga, aromatherapy, and the use of herbal remedies, Ayurvedic treatment takes on board the needs of individual body types or constitutions. Food is chosen, cooked, and eaten according to the season, the time of day, and the energies, tastes, flavors, and physical properties of the food itself. The aim is to create at all times the optimum conditions under which the body can extract as much benefit from food as possible.

Medical herbalism

Medical herbalism is the most ancient system of medicine, and has been used at some point in the evolution of every major culture as its main or only source of medicine. Although approaches differ, the governing principle is that of synergism — the strength of the sum of the parts is greater than that of the individual parts. Herbalists believe it is the combination of the active components of the plant which gives each its particular healing properties and helps prevent harmful side-effects. Herbalists, therefore, use the whole plant rather than isolating chemically active components, as in orthodox medicine.

The use of plants as medicine can be traced back to the Ancient Egyptians, whose priests were also practicing herbalists, and to the Ancient Greeks who were known to have compiled the earliest medical herbals. Herbal prescriptions dating back to 1500 BC have been found in China, and for centuries Indian Ayurvedic doctors have used herbs as a vital support to foods. The use of herbs spread across Europe with the Roman army; military doctors took healing plants with them to treat casualties. Knowledge of herbs also came from the Arabs via Spain and the Moorish invasions.

Early herbalism was often based on superstition, but there was real knowledge too. Hippocrates (460-377 BC), a widely traveled Greek practitioner, was so knowledgeable about the properties of plants and food that he became known as "the father of medicine." He taught that there were four "humors" or energies within the body — blood, phlegm, black bile, and yellow bile — and that any disturbance in the balance of the humors would result in ill health. Galen (AD 131-200), another respected herbalist, believed there were four key personalities — cheerful, sluggish, gloomy, and hot-tempered. Herbs were thought to have similar attributes and were prescribed to correct imbalances. The practice of medical herbalism became even more widespread following the invention of printing. One of the most renowned 17th-century herbalists was England's Nicholas Culpeper, whose hugely popular book, *Culpeper's Complete Herbal*, is still in print today. Another was master surgeon John Gerard, an enthusiastic botanist and respected physician whose herbal was used as a household bible. Once conventional medicine and surgery started to develop, herbalism took a back seat, but it is now enjoying something of a revival as people look for a safe way of healing without the side-effects of modern drugs.

The American tradition
The tradition of herbal medicine has always been strong in North America, thanks to the pooling of European and Native American skills. When the first European settlers arrived in the 18th and 19th centuries, the friendlier Indian tribes introduced the settlers to countless medicinal and culinary herbs which were unknown in Europe. The settlers, in turn, planted the seeds and roots of the herbs which they had brought with them from their native lands.

The North American Natives based their concept of medicine on the Great Spirit and the Medicine Wheel, within which they believe all humans are born and travel through life's journey. The Wheel is made up of Four Directions, each with its particular qualities and energies. Herbs are used as guides and as an aid to healing. Many of the Native American healing practices were centered around purification, not just of the body but also the spirit. Heat was considered a great purifier, and "hot" herbs were administered to induce violent vomiting. Sweating out body toxins in a sweat lodge was an essential ritual for curing disease, maintaining health, and preparing the body for enlightenment. Herbs were burned during the ceremony, and the smoke created was believed to be a link with the spirit world. For modern Native Americans, living on reservations, the use of herbs and traditional healing methods are vitally important and are used in preference to orthodox medicine.

Nature cures
The 19th century in Europe and North America saw a boom in natural healing techniques based on a strict dietary regime supported by various treatments and moderate exercise. Most of these techniques were founded on Hippocrates' principle of "first do no harm," suggesting that the body will heal itself, given sufficient time, and that cures should be as natural and non-invasive as possible.

In the early part of the century, the German therapist Vincent Preissnitz developed hydrotherapy, founded on his belief in the healing powers of water. Together with a simple diet of whole-wheat bread and vegetables, he prescribed energizing treatments such as sitz-baths, hot and cold showers, ice-cold compresses, wet packs, and steam treatments. Later, a Bavarian monk used a similar treatment on an ailing American, Benedict Lust, who, after a period of study, returned home to the United States to found his own version of the cure, now known as naturopathy. Food is a key issue for naturopaths, who believe that natural healing processes cannot work unless the diet is a healthy one. Another American movement, the Natural Hygienists, devised treatments using hydrotherapy and a hitherto unheard of diet of whole grains and vegetables. They also invented granola, one of the earliest breakfast cereals.

Mangez vivant!

Roughly translated as "Eat living food!," these were the words with which the Swiss doctor, Max Bircher-Brenner, advised patients at his sanitarium near Zurich. Towards the end of the 19th century, Dr Bircher-Brenner had discovered the joys of Preissnitz's wet-packs as a cure for insomnia, and in a period of ill health had felt better after regularly eating slices of raw apple. He had also successfully treated a patient suffering from digestive problems with a mix of raw fruit purée, honey, and goat's milk. Not content with the evidence, Dr Bircher-Brenner went on to spend many years conducting scientific investigations into the curative powers of raw foods. Meanwhile, he and his wife established a successful sanitarium named The Life Force, to which patients flocked for the healing diet of raw, fresh foods.

Early nutritional science

Food has always been an integral part of traditional healing practices. Despite this long-standing knowledge, the science of nutrition — the study of what happens to our food and the effect it has on us after we have swallowed it — did not receive much attention from the medical profession until the beginning of the 20th century, and even then it was not taken entirely seriously. During the 19th century, scientists worked out the chemical composition of organic and mineral substances, and the difference between inert and living matter. They also discovered that proteins were involved in

cell formation and repair, and that carbohydrates and fats provided the energy needed for life. In 1842, a German doctor, Julius von Mayer, developed the concept of the calorie as a measurement of energy.

In 1901 in Java, a Dutch doctor noticed his chickens were displaying symptoms of a deficiency disease normally found among people who eat only polished rice. Correctly guessing the cause, the doctor added rice bran to the chicken feed and the symptoms gradually cleared up. Attempts to identify the chemical nature of the disease-preventing constituent revealed that it belonged to a group of substances known as amines. In 1912, a Polish doctor suggested they be named "vitamines" — vital amines; the final 'e' was eventually dropped in English. Investigation of this exciting new topic was interrupted by the First World War, but from 1920 onward, the identification, isolation, and synthesizing of vitamins formed a major part of nutritional and biochemical research.

> ## ~ Muesli ~
> Dr Bircher-Brenner's patients at his sanitorium particularly enjoyed the muesli served at breakfast. This was a revolutionary food at the time but, thanks to the Swiss doctor, it now appears on breakfast tables throughout Europe. Bircher-Brenner's version was made with raw oatmeal soaked overnight in water and mixed with milk and a little fresh lemon juice. This was topped with grated, unpeeled apple and chopped nuts. Bircher-Brenner discovered muesli by chance from a 70 year-old Swiss shepherd whom he met on a mountain walk. The shepherd had eaten it for breakfast and dinner every day of his life and claimed he had not had a moment's illness.

MODERN HEALING AND HEALTHY EATING

Plants as medicine

In Ancient Egypt, Pliny made therapeutic use of cabbages, onions, garlic, and broccoli; the Romans swore by lentils, raisins, and grapes; and the Greeks had great faith in the healing powers of wine. Modern science is now proving what the early healers already knew — that everyday plant foods such as carrots, apples, sage, and onions, are rich in pharmacological substances which act in healing ways. They range from anticoagulants and cholesterol-reducers to immune-system boosters and cancer-blockers; and they can be as effective as any drug prescribed by a doctor.

Even the biggest pharmaceutical companies now devote a large part of their research programs to developing new drugs from plants, and at least 25% of common prescription drugs are also derived from them. For instance, a recent breakthrough for the Sandoz company was Cyclosporin A, derived from a certain type of fungus and now the major transplant surgery drug used to prevent the body from rejecting a newly implanted organ. Studies show that medicines made with extracts from the gingko biloba tree may enhance blood flow to the brain, which may have some effect on symptoms such as dizziness, depression, tinnitus, and short-term memory loss. They may also aid circulation in the legs and relieve cramps. Garlic is processed into a drug used for lowering blood cholesterol levels, while nicotinic acid is a highly effective drug used as a lipid-lowering mechanism for hypercholesterolemia.

Modern nutritional research

In its early days, the scope of human nutritional science did not go much beyond the study of physiological and biochemical processes. Today it covers such issues as:

♣ the role of food and nutrients in causing, preventing, and curing disease

♣ the effect on human health of too little or too much food, or of particular nutrients

♣ the importance of nutrition in the way we function as a whole — our mental and athletic performances, our resistance to infection, and so on

♣ ways of improving our eating habits

♣ the factors which make us choose certain foods and not others, even when we have been advised that doing so may pose a danger to our health.

Nutrition is a constantly evolving science, and fads seem to come and go overnight. However, there are currently two key areas which form the focus of modern research into the healing power of foods: antioxidants and essential fatty acids.

Antioxidants

The study of antioxidant nutrients has become one of the fastest-growing areas of nutritional research. It all points to the same conclusion: people who eat large amounts of fruits and vegetables have a hugely reduced risk of stroke, cataracts, certain cancers, and heart disease compared with those who do not. The same health benefits are not achieved by vitamin supplements in place of a fruit- and vegetable-rich diet. As more is learnt about antioxidants, scientists are beginning to understand that different types work selectively in different parts of the body. The most common are beta-carotene, the vitamins C and E, and the minerals selenium, zinc, manganese, and copper, but new ones are constantly being studied. Antioxidants in the limelight are vitamin E, bioflavonoids, carotenoids — particularly beta-carotene — and glutathione.

Bioflavonoids These occur widely in fruits and vegetables, particularly citrus fruits, blackcurrants (a member of the gooseberry family widely grown in Europe), and dark-green leaf vegetables. Vast numbers of bioflavonoids have been identified and their antioxidant properties are continually being studied. Quercetin, found in cabbages, green tea, and apple peel, is believed to be a powerful anti-inflammatory, anti-viral, and anti-tumor agent. A deficiency may contribute to hay fever, asthma, and skin diseases such as eczema and psoriasis. Combined with vitamin C, quercetin may also help prevent infections such as the common cold. High concentrations of another type of bioflavonoid, the polyphenols or polyphenolic bioflavonoids, have been found in some tree barks and teas, as well as in red wine, which may account for the recently acclaimed health benefits. Research suggests that pycnogenol, found in pine bark, may help delay skin aging by strengthening the collagen.

Many of the research findings on the healing properties of bioflavonoids — only some of which we have touched on — have yet to be substantiated, but they offer hope that additional research will provide an insight into their role in good health.

Carotenoids These occur mainly in orange- and red-fleshed fruits and vegetables, and also in dark-green leafy vegetables. Carotenoids are primarily found in the form of beta-carotene in nature, and this is one of the most effective antioxidants of all the carotenoids. There is substantial evidence that beta-carotene can stimulate the immune system and decrease the risk of certain cancers. Researchers are just beginning to realize the pharmacological importance of carotenoids other than beta-carotene. Currently receiving attention is lycopene, found in tomatoes and tomato products. A study reported in the American Journal of the National Cancer Institute suggests that lycopene significantly reduces the risk of prostate cancer. Other studies have shown that lycopene also reduces the risk of endometrial, breast, and cervical cancers. Lutein, found in broccoli, cabbage, and spinach, is another carotenoid receiving attention. It is thought to offer particular protection to the macula — the part of the retina that distinguishes fine detail in the central field of vision — and thus has implications for degenerative eye conditions.

Glutathione Another antioxidant receiving attention, made in the body from three amino-acids, glutamate, cysteine, and glycine. Fresh meat is an excellent source, fruits and vegetables contain moderate amounts, while dairy products, bread, and cereals contain only a little.

Essential fatty acids

Current research focuses on two major categories of polyunsaturated fatty acids — omega-3 and omega-6 — known as essential fatty acids, since the body cannot make them for itself and they must be provided in the diet. Factors such as stress, excess alcohol, high cholesterol levels, aging, and diabetes can cause deficiencies.

Omega-3 fatty acids These fatty acids, derived from linolenic acid, are found in oily fish such as sardines, mackerel, herring, salmon, tuna, haddock, and weakfish, as well as in soybean and canola oils, and walnuts. Extensive research into the Eskimo diet has found a strong correlation between a high intake of fish and other forms of seafood and a low incidence of heart disease. Clinical trials have shown that as little as 4 ounces per week of oily fish will provide reasonable protection against heart disease. Reports also claim that fish oils help protect against hypertension, psoriasis, migraine, eczema, and rheumatism. They can also lower blood cholesterol and triglycerides. Different ways of incorporating fish oils into the Western diet are constantly being

devised, for instance in bread, milk, yogurt, and even infant formula feed.

Omega-6 fatty acids These are derived from linoleic acid, and are found in vegetable oils such as sunflower, safflower, corn, and soybean oils. Linoleic acid is an essential part of the diet since it is converted in the body to arachidonic acid — an indispensable constituent of certain cell membranes, particularly those of the nervous system. Arachidonic acid is, in turn, converted into eicosanoids, which help control a wide variety of cell functions including blood-clot formation and inflammation, as well as aiding the control of cardiovascular hemostasis.

We need about 4 grams of omega-6 fatty acids per day — about 2 teaspoons of sunflower oil or a handful of almonds or walnuts. More than this may offer some protection against heart disease, but excessive amounts may be harmful, since they increase the production of free radicals.

HEALTHY EATING PRACTICES

Twenty years ago, the idea of healthy eating was largely of minority interest; nowadays there is widespread recognition that diet and health are interconnected, and that if we eat unwisely we run risks. Scientific evidence gathered by the World Health Organization, comparing diets and diseases throughout the world, all points in the same direction. Eating the right foods not only helps prevent the "diseases of affluence," such as coronary heart disease, tooth decay, and obesity, but can also protect against several kinds of

cancer, including breast cancer and colon cancer. What we eat also affects our chance of suffering from high blood pressure and strokes, osteoporosis (brittle bones), diabetes in middle age, and a host of other common illnesses.

Patterns for protection

In 1990, the World Health Organization recommended a simple healthy eating pattern to protect against the diseases of affluence and promote good health.

Food was divided into three groups:

❧ bread, potatoes, and cereals

❧ vegetables, salads, and fruits

❧ meat, fish, and dairy foods

The first group makes up the greater part of the diet, with group two following close behind. Meat, fish, and dairy products take a back seat. The basic message still stands but has been refined still further. The United States Department of Agriculture has replaced the simple groupings with a seven-section food pyramid. Bread, cereals, rice, and pasta form the base of the pyramid and should make up more than half your daily diet. The next level up is divided between vegetables (3-5 servings a day) and fruits (2-4 servings). On a higher level still, there is milk, yogurt, and cheese (2-3 servings) and protein foods — meats, poultry, fish, and eggs (2-3 servings). Fats, oils, and sugars form the tip of the pyramid and are to be eaten in small quantities.

In the United Kingdom, a similar pattern is based on a five-section pie-chart devised by the Department of Health, the Ministry of Agriculture, Fisheries, and Food, and the Health Education Authority. The pattern follows the same basic groupings with bread, other cereals, and potatoes making up one-third of the diet, and fruits and vegetables making up a second third. In the remaining third, meats, fish, and alternatives, and milk and dairy foods form equal parts, while foods containing fat and/or sugar form the smallest segment.

Diets around the world

Researchers are constantly evaluating different diets from around the world. It is now evident that there is far less incidence of the "diseases of affluence" in countries where the diet as a whole contains less meat, fat, and dairy products.

Mediterranean One of the healthiest and perhaps the easiest to adopt is the Mediterranean diet. High in antioxidants from fish, fruits, and vegetables and low in saturated fats, the diet evolved due to poverty, location, and climate. Commonly used ingredients such as tomatoes and olives are cheap to produce and thrive in the dry heat, while the sea is a generous provider of fish. Meat is scarce, expensive, and often tough. The cooking medium is olive oil, which is high in monounsaturated fatty acids that do not clog up the arteries. Convincing evidence has begun to emerge that eating along these lines can help prevent heart disease and some cancers.

Latin American Hot, exotic, and spicy, the staple foods in this diet are complex carbohydrates — maize, beans, and rice. People eat plenty of vegetables and fresh fruits, all rich in antioxidants, and little meat or dairy produce. Most Latin American peoples have a low incidence of heart disease and cancers — a factor believed to be diet-related. Unsurprisingly, in the beef-rearing countries of the eastern seaboard — Brazil, Argentina, and Uruguay — there is a higher incidence of heart disease.

Japanese and South-East Asian Across the Pacific in Japan, China, Malaysia, Indonesia, and the Philippines, the diet is generally based on fish, white meats, vegetables, and rice, but with regional and national differences. Japan has been influenced by centuries of Buddhism, which advocates vegetarianism. Antioxidant-rich vegetables are a key feature, as are rice and fish. The incidence of heart disease and breast cancer is low in most southeast Asian countries. In Japan, however, the incidence of stomach cancer is higher than in the West, and the evidence points to the nitrates in pickled and cured vegetables and fish, which are eaten on a regular basis.

Indian Although Indian food varies from region to region and is as strongly influenced by religion as it is by geography, the diet throughout the country is built on sound dietary principles. Complex carbohydrates, such as rice or wheat flatbreads, are the main component, while other foods are looked upon as an accompaniment. Vegetables play a dominant role, since most of the population are non-meat-eating Hindus. Protein is more often derived from pulses and dairy products than meats, so the diet is relatively low in saturated fats. Spices and seasonings are carefully chosen along Ayurvedic principles in order to physically and spiritually fine-tune the body.

Middle Eastern The diet in most Middle Eastern countries dates back to ancient principles which stated that there must be perfect harmony between the elements of the universe and the human body. As far back as the 11th century, Arab doctors recommended vegetables, rice, beans, and meats as the ideal food combinations. The modern diet is based on the same principles. Wheat is the staple food and fresh vegetables, whole grains, and all kinds of fruits play a major part. Meat is eaten in moderate amounts.

Balkan The Balkan people are famed for their longevity, which has been attributed to widespread consumption of "live" yogurt and hunza apricots. They also enjoy a low rate of heart disease and diet-related cancers thanks to a diet high in whole grains, vegetables, and fruits, and low in meat and meat products. Vegetables and fruits are often eaten raw, which minimizes the loss of valuable nutrients.

Different diets used in the West
In a search for improved health, many people in the West adopt diets which differ from a conventional meat-based one.

Vegetarian and vegan diets There is no doubt that vegetarians tend to have a better health record than meat-eaters. However, this may be related to lifestyle, so it is difficult to link their good health with diet alone. A survey carried out by the University of Texas showed that many vegetarians abstained from alcohol and smoking, many took vitamin supplements, and a disproportionate number practiced meditation and relaxation techniques. Vegetarians and vegans tend to eat more complex carbohydrates and fiber than meat-eaters, and fewer saturated fats. Provided the balance of nutrients is correct, the diet is obviously a healthy one since evidence shows that vegetarians usually have lower blood cholesterol, which means lower rates of heart disease, lower blood pressure, less incidence of colon cancer, fewer bowel problems, and less incidence of

osteoporosis in women. Vegetarians also have a lower risk of developing gall stones and diverticular disease. Some nutritionists feel that although a vegetarian diet can sustain an adult in good health, it is not necessarily appropriate for infants and young children. Growing children need plenty of the high-calorie foods normally provided by fats, and their stomachs may be too small to cope with large quantities of bulky carbohydrate foods needed to provide energy. Since vegans do not eat eggs or dairy products, it is particularly important for them to find alternative sources of essential nutrients such as calcium, iron, vitamin D, and vitamin B12, otherwise deficiencies are likely to occur.

Macrobiotic diet Founded by Japanese George Ohsawa, macrobiotics spread to the West in the early 1950s. The diet is based on the Chinese system of balancing yin and yang foods. Yin foods are characterized by acidity, potassium, sugar, and fruits; yang foods by alkalinity and sodium. In terms of energy intake, the diet is very much in line with current recommendations: 55-75% complex carbohydrates (grains, pulses, and starchy vegetables), 15-30% fat, and 10-15% protein. In its early days, brown rice was promoted as the perfectly balanced food — a concept severely at odds with Western nutritional thinking. Many macrobiotic enthusiasts overemphasized the importance of brown rice in the diet, resulting in several cases of severe malnutrition. Although still based on whole grains, the diet is now much more balanced and includes plenty of vegetables, sea vegetables, soups, seeds, nuts, fruits, and even a small amount of fish.

The Hay diet According to the Hay diet, the body cannot simultaneously digest protein and starchy carbohydrates, or carbohydrates and acidic fruits. Foods from these groups are therefore eaten separately. The creator of this diet, Dr William Hay, believed that by following these principles, the body's own natural healing powers would be enhanced. There is no scientific evidence to support his theory, but thousands of people claim to have benefited from following the Hay diet. They say they feel more clear-headed and energetic, lose weight without trying, and suffer few digestive problems. The diet is said to improve conditions such as arthritis, asthma, and hay fever.

Raw food diet Like the Hay diet, followers of a raw food diet extol its virtues, claiming that it improves vitality, encourages weight loss, and helps the system to detoxify. They believe that cooking and processing not only destroys nutrients but also depletes the health-giving properties of foods. The diet is largely based on fruits, vegetables, and nuts, so provides plenty of antioxidants, fiber, potassium, and a little protein. Small amounts of dairy produce and oil are allowed, even though these foods have been processed. Energy-boosting carbohydrates such as beans, pasta, rice, and potatoes are excluded since they cannot be eaten raw. The diet is likely to be deficient in iron, since it excludes meat and pulses, and may be deficient in calcium, vitamin B12, and protein. Excessive amounts of raw food can lead to irritable bowel syndrome. The diet is not suitable for young children, or people such as pregnant women or cancer sufferers who need to maintain their weight.

Diets for Western lifestyles

The hectic pace of life in the 1990s, combined with the hazards of environmental pollution, mean that we are more reliant than ever on the healing power of foods to keep us in peak condition and to ward off disease. Sometimes we need to modify the diet in order to cope with life's demands.

Anti-stress diet As long as stressful experiences do not occur too frequently, most of us can cope without any serious ill effects. Excessive or prolonged stress, however, can be intolerable and needs to be dealt with. You may not be able to eliminate or reduce the stress in your life, but you can improve your ability to cope with it. It is vital to set aside times for rest and relaxation. Exercise — even taking a short walk — deep breathing and awareness practices, such as meditation, yoga, and t'ai chi, are all effective ways of clearing the mind and recharging the body's batteries.

When you are under stress, the body consumes more nutrients, so it is essential to try and eat well even though this may be the last thing you feel like doing. A way of overcoming stress-induced loss of appetite is to eat small, infrequent meals and healthy snacks. Excessive amounts of tea and coffee may temporarily stimulate the body, but they will also serve to increase your anxiety levels — as will alcohol.

Energy-boosting diet We all need energy just so that the body can perform its normal biological processes, but the exact amount depends on many factors including sex, age, build, basal metabolic rate, as well as the climate in which you live, the type of work

---

**Stress-busting
~ foods ~**

B *vitamins* to release energy from food and maintain a healthy nervous system. Found in whole grains, green vegetables, eggs, pulses, nuts, seeds, dried fruits, meats, poultry, and fish.

Vitamin C to help resist infection. Found in fresh fruits, especially citrus fruits, strawberries, and kiwifruits.

Zinc to help resist infection. Found in egg yolk, dairy produce, liver, red meats, oysters, and seafood.

Complex carbohydrates to boost energy levels. Found in whole grains, whole-wheat bread, pasta, root vegetables, and potatoes.

---

you do, and how much exercise you take. A healthy, varied diet should provide plenty of energy, but you will need to boost supplies if you have a physically demanding job, work long hours, are undergoing prolonged stress, or if you exercise on a regular basis.

The energy in our food is bound up in carbohydrates, fats, and proteins. The energy in food also depends on water content; food with a high water content, such as clear soup, has a lower energy value, while densely textured foods, such as bananas, have a higher energy value. Carbohydrates and fats provide most of the energy required for physical activity and exercise. Energy from protein is used only when the body's supply of carbohydrates and fats is used up.

Although fats provide more than twice the amount of energy than carbohydrates, carbohydrates are the most important fuel for exercise. If you exercise vigorously, you will also need extra minerals such as calcium, potassium, magnesium, and zinc.

~ Energy boosters ~

Breakfast cereals with added dried fruits or bananas.

Whole-wheat bread — thick slices spread with peanut butter and/or bananas.

Rice or pasta — large portions served with a meat- or vegetable-based sauce.

Baked beans on whole-wheat toast.

Large baked potatoes topped with yogurt or grated cheese.

Whole-wheat fruit cakes and bars — choose low-sugar, low-fat varieties.

Mineral-rich foods

Calcium is found in dairy products and dark-green leaf vegetables.

Potassium is found in lean meats, vegetables, nuts, pulses, and fruits, especially bananas.

Magnesium is found in seafood, dark-green leafy vegetables, whole grains, nuts, and pulses.

Zinc is found in seafood, variety meats, eggs, wheat germ, and pulses.

Exclusion diet Used to pinpoint the cause of food intolerances and allergies, an exclusion diet involves excluding one or more foods for a period of time, usually two weeks, and then reintroducing the food to observe the effect. Patients often feel worse for the first week or so, as withdrawal symptoms make themselves felt, but after that there is usually an improvement in well-being. Such diets should be followed under strict medical and dietetic supervision, and only when a good reason for doing so has been established.

Food choices

The food we eat and the cultural, political, and economic influences that affect our choice have a direct effect on our health. Food has never been more diverse and difficult to judge in terms of quality, nutritional status, and wholesomeness. Seasons have become relatively meaningless, traditionally reared meats, poultry, and fish are now produced on factory farms, bread is churned out from computerized bakeries, and tasteless, uniformly-shaped vegetables grow in serried ranks in glasshouses.

That said, a growing number of producers are returning to, or are determinedly holding on to, sound traditional practices of careful animal husbandry, using traditional craftsmanship to make all manner of foods — bread, cheese, preserves, cured meats — and rediscovering varieties of fruits and vegetables that actually taste of something. By becoming aware of what is available and demanding good-quality, soundly produced, health-promoting foods, consumers have the collective power to keep these producers in business and to improve the quality of the foods served up to us by the supermarkets.

Making the most ~ of food ~

Relaxation Eastern cultures state that a sense of enjoyment opens our bodies to the nourishment provided by the food; in the West, we would say that if we are relaxed, the digestive process works better. It all amounts to the same thing. It is best to eat when we are not distracted or troubled by other influences, so try not to read or watch television or take phone calls during a meal. Taking a few deep breaths before eating is a good way of relaxing, and sitting quietly for a few minutes after a meal is a sure-fire aid to digestion.

Posture How you sit makes a difference too. Eating hunched up or with crossed legs hinders the progress of food through the system.

Chewing It is worth remembering the Chinese saying which states: "The stomach has no teeth." Well-chewed food places less stress on the digestive organs and helps increase the absorption of nutrients.

Stop eating Be aware of how full you are and stop eating before you reach that point. Eating more than you need stresses the digestive system. You end up feeling tired because all your energy has gone into the digestive process.

Relaxation and enjoyment of food

Our health and well-being are not only affected by our choice of foods, but also our frame of mind when preparing them. Eastern cultures believe that the life-force chi is transferred between people in interactions of every sort, and the chi of the cook permeates the food. On a less spiritual level, most of us have experienced the difference in meals prepared calmly with a sense of enjoyment. The food simply tastes better. On the other hand, if we are in a hurry or feeling bad-tempered when we cook, the meal can be dull or downright disastrous.

Meal schedules

A health-promoting meal schedule is a matter of personal choice. Some people prefer only one or two meals a day, while most of us are used to three. The Chinese, who believe that the body's digestive organs have peak activity during two-hour intervals, normally have five small meals a day. Ideally, the day should begin with a low-fat, energy-boosting breakfast, the main meal should be taken at lunchtime so that we have time to digest it, and the final meal of the day should be relatively light.

Gentle
Awakenings

BREAKFASTS AND EARLY MORNING DRINKS

Breakfast, however simple, can be an enjoyable and therapeutic ritual. Taking time for it, rather than running around in a frantic state, creates a sense of order, and it gives you the chance to calmly contemplate the hours ahead.

When we sleep the body becomes dehydrated, so on waking one of the first needs to be satisfied is thirst. If you wake feeling clear-headed and alert, a light herb tea or a glass of hot water with a slice of lemon is usually all that's needed. Feeling sluggish or muzzy-headed on waking is a sign that digestion may be incomplete, perhaps because you ate late the night before or the meal was high in protein. In this case, a fruit or vegetable juice, or a stronger type of herb tea, would be a good choice.

Breakfast usually follows a long period of fasting during sleep, so it is important to refuel. If you venture out without doing so, you are more likely to feel lethargic and jaded by mid-morning. However, we are all individuals, and while some people may only be able to get through the morning if they have breakfasted well, others may be unable to face anything too solid at this time of day. You don't have to eat a substantial breakfast, but do eat a sustaining one. Breakfast can consist of anything you like, but the bare essentials are a whole grain — either in breakfast cereal or whole-wheat toast — or fresh fruit, or a small pot of plain yogurt.

In the chapter that follows, you'll find refreshing and nutritious ideas for drinks and breakfasts to suit all appetites and tastes.

~ Herb teas ~

Herb teas have been drunk
for thousands of years. They
can be taken for therapeutic
reasons or simply enjoyed
for their refreshing flavors.
The main advantage is that
herbal teas do not contain
caffeine, and so offer a
pleasant and healthful
alternative to tea and
coffee. They can also help
cleanse, calm, or stimulate
the body in a gentle but
effective way, and can be
taken according to your
need, mood, and season.
Teas made with freshly
gathered herbs have a
clean, bright flavor, but you
can also use dried herbs,
either loose or packaged.
You will need a small
handful of fresh herbs
(leaves, flowers, or stems)
or 2 teaspoons of dried
herbs per cup of boiling
water. If you want a stronger
tea, add more herbs rather
than leaving the tea to
steep for longer. It is
important to cover the tea
while brewing, so that the
health-giving properties
are not carried away
in the steam.

Lemon Herb Tea

Used singly or in combination, lemony herbs such
as lemon balm, lemongrass, lemon verbena, and
bergamot make a wonderfully refreshing but gentle
tea which, unlike some early morning herb blends,
isn't too much of a shock to the system.

• S E R V E S   1 - 2 •
Preparation time: 5 minutes
good handful of fresh lemon balm, lemon verbena,
or bergamot leaves, or a mixture
1-2 lemongrass leaves or stalks, bruised

🌿 Rinse the leaves very briefly if you are worried
about dirt or insect life. Put them in a two-cup
teapot.
🌿 Pour on boiling water and cover. Leave to brew
for 5 minutes, then strain into a cup.

Ginger and Mint Tea

Ginger and mint both have a stimulating aroma and
settle the stomach. Ginger is known to reduce
motion sickness and associated nausea.

• S E R V E S   1 - 2 •
Preparation time: 5 minutes
Cooking time: 5 minutes, plus 5 minutes infusing
a good handful of fresh mint leaves
1-inch piece fresh ginger root, peeled
and thinly sliced

🌿 Briefly rinse the mint leaves if necessary and
put in a two-cup teapot.
🌿 Put the ginger in a small saucepan with 2½
cups of water. Cover and boil for 5 minutes. Pour
the liquid over the mint and cover. Leave to infuse
for 5 minutes, then strain into a cup.

Hot Pear Juice with Cardamom

If you like to start the day with fruit juice, try hot or
warm pear juice rather than chilled citrus juice.
Being less acidic, it is kinder to an empty stomach.

• S E R V E S   2 •
Preparation time: 5 minutes
Cooking time: 5 minutes
4 tablespoons pear juice concentrate
seeds from 4 green cardamom pods

🌿 Pour 2 tablespoons of pear juice concentrate
into two 1¼-cup mugs or heatproof glasses.
🌿 Lightly crush the cardamom seeds and put in a
small saucepan with 2½ cups of water. Cover and
boil for 5 minutes. Strain the liquid over the pear
juice concentrate, stirring to dissolve.

~ Nuts ~

Doctor Kellogg, originator of Kellogg's breakfast cereals, once referred to nuts as "the choicest product of nature's laboratory." Nuts are an excellent source of vitamin E — one of the antioxidants — and a valuable source of protein. They also contain a limited amount of B vitamins and iron. They are a useful source of zinc and have a high potassium and magnesium content but are often low in calcium. All nuts are low in sodium unless, of course, you eat them salted. Most nuts also contain selenium, a valuable trace mineral linked to lower rates of heart disease and cancer — brazil nuts are a particularly good source. A drawback with nuts is that they have a high fat content (although it is the healthy, unsaturated kind), so go easy if you are counting the calories. However, they do contain linoleic acid, an essential fatty acid thought to counteract the build-up of blood cholesterol.

Toasted Nut Granola in Fruit Juice

Fragrant toasted nuts and coconut ribbons add a touch of luxury to this energy-boosting, European-style breakfast. Store in an airtight container and use as required.

Soaking granola in fruit juice makes it easier to digest and also quenches an early morning thirst more effectively than milk.

• MAKES 10-12 SERVINGS •
Preparation time: 20 minutes
Cooking time: 10 minutes, plus 6 hours soaking
6 *tablespoons coconut ribbons or flakes*
2 *tbsp filberts*
2 *tablespoons almonds*
2 *tablespoons shelled pumpkin seeds (pepitas)*
2 *tablespoons shelled sunflower seeds*
5 *cups raw oatmeal or rolled oats*
½ *cup raisins*
6 *tablespoons finely chopped dried apples*
3 *tablespoons finely chopped dried apricots*
pear juice or apple juice concentrate, for soaking

🍄 Preheat the oven to 350°. Put the coconut ribbons on a baking tray and the filberts and almonds together on another tray. Toast the coconut ribbons for 3-4 minutes and the nuts for 5-7 minutes, stirring occasionally, until golden-brown. Be careful not to let them burn.
🍄 Rub the skins off the filberts with a clean kitchen towel, then chop them with the almonds.
🍄 Mix the nuts and coconut ribbons with the seeds, oats, raisins, apple, and apricots.
🍄 Put the required amount of granola in a small bowl or plastic container. Pour enough weakly diluted pear or apple juice concentrate over it to barely cover it. Cover with a lid and leave for at least 6 hours or overnight before serving.

Wheatflake Bars with Bananas and Fresh Orange Juice

If you don't like milk, breakfast cereals may not be part of your diet. However, they are rich in carbohydrates and make an energy-boosting start to the day. Here's a way of serving them without milk.

• SERVES 1 •
Preparation time: 5 minutes, plus soaking
2 *wheatflake bars (e.g. Weetabix) or shredded wheat*
2-3 oranges
1 *small banana, sliced*
wholemilk plain organic yogurt, to serve (optional)

🍄 Put the wheatflake bars or shredded wheat in a serving bowl. Thoroughly squeeze the oranges and strain the juice over the cereal. You will need about ½ cup of orange juice.
🍄 Top with sliced banana and a spoonful of creamy wholemilk yogurt if you like.

VARIATIONS

🍄 Replace the filberts with brazil nuts, or try using unsalted cashews on their own.
🍄 Top with sliced fresh fruit such as strawberries, bananas, or grapes.

Warm Dried Fruit Compôte with Sweet Couscous

• SERVES 4 •

Preparation time: 15 minutes, plus soaking

Cooking time: 10 minutes

½ cup prunes

2 tablespoons dried apricots

3 tablespoons dried peaches

2 tablespoons dried pears

2 tablespoons dried apple rings

finely grated zest of 1 lemon and 1 orange

brown sugar or honey (optional), to serve

FOR THE COUSCOUS:

1 cup semi-skim milk or water

1 tablespoon raisins

crushed seeds from 2 cardamom pods

¼ teaspoon freshly grated nutmeg

½ cup instant couscous

Wash the fruit and cut the bigger pieces in half. Put in a bowl with 2½ cups of water and the lemon and orange zest. Leave to soak for 4-6 hours or overnight, stirring occasionally.

Pour the fruit and the soaking liquid into a saucepan. Bring to the boil, then simmer for 5-8 minutes, until soft. Pour into a serving bowl with the juices.

Meanwhile, pour the milk or water into a saucepan and add the raisins, cardamom, and nutmeg. Bring to the boil, pour in the couscous, and lower the heat. Stir for 30 seconds, then remove from the heat and leave to stand, covered, for 7-8 minutes, until the liquid has been absorbed.

Divide the couscous between individual serving bowls. Top with the fruit and the cooking juices, adding a little sugar or honey if necessary to sweeten.

Buckwheat Pancakes

These quickly made pancakes are delicious served with blueberries, raspberries, or warm apple sauce.

Buckwheat is an excellent source of fiber, B vitamins, copper, iron, and vitamin E. Buckwheat flour does not contain gluten and is therefore particularly useful if you suffer from celiac disease. However, this recipe also contains all-purpose flour.

• MAKES 20 •

Preparation time: 5 minutes

Cooking time: 15 minutes

¾ cup buckwheat flour

¾ cup all-purpose flour

1 tsp sugar

½ teaspoon baking powder

½ teaspoon baking soda

¼ teaspoon salt

1½ cups buttermilk

1 large egg, beaten

1 tablespoon grapeseed or safflower oil

honey, plain wholemilk yogurt, and fresh berries or warm apple sauce, to serve

Combine all the dry ingredients in a bowl. Beat in the buttermilk, egg, and oil.

Place a griddle or heavy-based skillet over medium-high heat and brush with a little oil. Stir the mixture, then pour 2 tablespoons onto the griddle, spreading it with the back of a metal spoon to form a 4-inch circle. Add 3 or 4 more circles, depending on the size of your pan.

Fry for 30 seconds, or until holes start to appear on the surface. Flip the pancakes over and fry on the other side for 30 seconds, or until golden-brown. Keep warm while you make the rest.

Top with a spoonful of yogurt and honey, and serve with fresh berries or warm apple sauce.

HEALING FOOD

~ Eggs ~

Eggs provide a good balance of vital nutrients. Inexpensive, easily digested, and adaptable to any meal, eggs are an excellent source of high biological value protein and a rich source of iron. Eggs are an excellent source of vitamin B12 — often lacking in a vegetarian diet. The lecithin in egg yolk is rich in choline, which helps transport cholesterol around the blood. The fatty acids in eggs are about 65% mono- and polyunsaturated, with only about 30% saturated. Egg yolk has a high cholesterol content, and because of this, many nutritional experts recommend an upper limit of four eggs per week. However, it is now known that the amount of total fat and saturated fats in the diet has more effect on raising blood cholesterol levels than the actual amount of cholesterol consumed. The World Health Organization recommends an upper limit of ten eggs per week from all sources.

Smoked Tofu Kedgeree
with Almonds

This makes an energy-giving weekend breakfast or brunch, or you could even serve it for supper. Tofu is low in fat, rich in calcium and magnesium, and a good source of first-class plant protein. Almonds add useful amounts of vitamin E, potassium, calcium, and magnesium.

This dish is also very delicious when cooked in the traditional way with smoked fish instead of tofu. If you cook it with fish, choose naturally-dyed fish which is creamy gold in color. Brilliant yellow fish could be dyed with azo dyes such as tartrazine or sunset yellow, which may cause an allergic reaction in some people.

• SERVES 4-6 •

Preparation time: 20 minutes
Cooking time: 40 minutes
1 cup long-grain brown rice
1 teaspoon salt
3 eggs
lump of butter
1 tablespoon grapeseed or safflower oil
1 cup smoked tofu, drained, pressed dry, and cut
into ¾-inch cubes
2 tablespoons flaked almonds
5 tablespoons chopped fresh chives or parsley
salt and freshly ground black pepper

🐾 Rinse the rice and place it in a saucepan with the salt and enough water to cover by the depth of your thumb. Bring to the boil, then cover tightly, and simmer over a very low heat for 30-40 minutes, until all the liquid is absorbed.

🐾 Meanwhile, put the eggs in a saucepan, cover with water, and bring to the boil. Boil for 5 minutes exactly, then remove from the heat and drain. Remove the shells and roughly chop the white and yolk.

🐾 Tip the rice into a warmed serving bowl, breaking up any lumps with a fork. Stir in the eggs and butter, and keep warm.

🐾 Heat the oil in a small pan and gently fry the tofu for a minute or two until heated through. Add it to the rice and eggs.

🐾 Fry the almonds until golden-brown and add them to the rice.

🐾 Stir in the chives and a little more butter if necessary. Season with salt and freshly ground black pepper.

VARIATION

🐾 To make the dish with smoked fish, such as whitefish, poach 1 pound of natural, undyed smoked fish for about 10 minutes in enough milk or water (or a mixture) to cover. Drain, reserving the poaching liquid, and flake the fish, discarding any skin and bones. Stir it into the rice mixture, adding some of the poaching liquid to moisten if you like.

A Lunchtime Lift

SOUPS AND LIGHT MEALS

Ideally, the midday meal should be the largest of the day so that the body has time to digest it properly. However, for many people this simply is not practical, especially during the working week. Nevertheless, even a light lunch needs to be sufficiently sustaining to keep your body and mind in good working order until evening. A bowl of soup and either a salad or a light savory dish will leave you feeling satisfied but not sluggish.

When making soups, the better the stock the better the soup. Home-made is best, even if it is simply the water from cooked vegetables. A well-prepared soup produces a definite feeling of well-being that can lift fatigue. It is easy to digest but still satisfying, and is just as suitable for solitary meals or for serving to a gathering. Similarly, a hearty salad composed of a variety of well-chosen ingredients can make a nutritionally balanced, satisfying meal that does not leave you feeling bloated.

However packed your schedule, don't be tempted simply to grab a sandwich and eat on the run. Your body will benefit far more if you stop what you're doing and take the time to enjoy your lunch — no matter how simple. Sitting quietly for five to ten minutes after eating will also give the body an opportunity to digest.

This chapter offers lively ideas for hearty soups, colorful salads, and appetizing savory dishes, many of which can be prepared ahead of time and used as part of a lunch to take to work.

HEALING FOOD

~ Miso ~

Miso is a naturally fermented soybean paste made with whole soybeans and cereal grains. It is one of the world's most versatile and health-promoting foods, brought to Japan from China about 2,500 years ago. It makes a nourishing addition to stews, bean dishes, sandwich fillings, sauces, and dressings. Unpasteurized miso is a "live" food containing lactic acid bacteria and enzymes that help the digestion. It should be added to hot dishes at the end of the cooking time and never boiled, otherwise the health-giving bacteria will be destroyed. Miso is a storehouse of vegetarian protein and essential vitamins and minerals. It is a rich source of vitamin A, potassium, sodium, calcium, and phosphorus. It also contains a trace of vitamin B12, often lacking in vegan diets. Research suggests that eating miso may help reduce the risk of breast cancer and cancer.

Miso Soup with Rice Noodles and Vegetables

Instant miso soup is one of the best convenience foods around. It's a godsend when you're traveling — just add boiling water and you have a healthful cup of additive-free nutrients. Light in flavor but fortifying, it's good if you have an upset stomach. This recipe includes additional rice noodles and fresh vegetables to make a more substantial soup.

• SERVES 4 •

Preparation time: 20 minutes
Cooking time: 10 minutes
1 teaspoon sesame seeds
1 quart water
3 ounces thin rice noodles, broken into 2-inch pieces
2 carrots, very finely diced
3 green onions (scallions), greens parts included,
sliced diagonally into ½-inch pieces
4 ounces watercress, stalks removed,
leaves roughly chopped
4 packages instant miso soup powder
tamari (Japanese soy sauce), to taste

❧ Put the sesame seeds in a small, heavy-based skillet without any oil. Dry-fry over medium-high heat, until they smell toasted and begin to turn color. Remove from the pan and set aside.

❧ Bring the water to the boil in a medium-large saucepan. Add the noodles, carrots, and green onions (scallions). Boil for 3-4 minutes or according to the instructions on the noodle package, separating the noodles with a fork. Add the watercress and boil for a few seconds, until wilted.

❧ Remove the pan from the heat and add the miso, stirring until dissolved. Pour into serving bowls and sprinkle with the toasted sesame seeds. Add a dash of tamari to taste.

Carrot and Coriander Soup

Carrots are rich in beta-carotene, one of the major antioxidants, and fresh coriander (cilantro) contains a fair amount too.

• SERVES 6 •

Preparation time: 25 minutes
Cooking time: 30 minutes
2 tablespoon butter
1 onion, minced
6 cups sliced carrots
1 cup sliced potatoes
2½ -3 pints vegetable or chicken broth,
preferably home-made
salt and freshly ground black pepper
1 large bunch fresh coriander (cilantro), about
4 ounces, stalks removed, leaves chopped
1 tablespoon lime juice
yogurt or sour cream and good bread, such as
Tomato and Pumpkin Seed Bread, page 34, to serve

❧ Melt the butter in a large saucepan. Add the onion, cover, and sweat over medium-low heat, until just soft. Add the carrots and potatoes, cover, and continue to cook for a further 10 minutes, stirring occasionally.

❧ Add 2½ pints of the broth, and season with salt and pepper. Bring to the boil, then cover and simmer for approximately 15 minutes, or until the vegetables are just soft.

❧ Pour the soup into a blender or food processor and blend until smooth. Pour it back into the saucepan, then add the coriander (cilantro), lime juice, and more broth if you think the soup is too thick. Reheat gently and check the seasoning.

❧ Ladle into warmed soup bowls and swirl in a spoonful of yogurt or sour cream. Serve with good fresh bread, such as Tomato and Pumpkin Seed Bread — see page 34.

Black Bean and Roasted Tomato Soup

This spicy, robust soup is a meal in itself — hardly surprising since pulses, such as black beans, are packed with protein, carbohydrate, and fiber. The beans also contain useful amounts of folate, one of the B vitamins, as well as iron, zinc, calcium, and magnesium. Avocado, chili, and lime add zingy freshness and color to the soup.

• SERVES 4 •

Preparation time: 30 minutes, plus soaking
Cooking time: 1 hour

¾ cup black turtle beans, soaked overnight
3 ripe plum tomatoes
1 small red onion, unpeeled
4 garlic cloves, unpeeled
1 tablespoon olive oil
2-3 sprigs fresh thyme
½ teaspoon black peppercorns, crushed
1 teaspoon coriander seeds, crushed
½ teaspoon cumin seeds, crushed
1 quart vegetable or chicken broth,
preferably home-made
salt

TO GARNISH:
2 tablespoons chopped fresh coriander
(cilantro) leaves
½ avocado, cubed and tossed in lime juice
1 small fresh red chili, seeded, and finely sliced
lime segments

🍄 Drain the beans, rinse well, and put in a saucepan with enough water to cover by about 2 inches. Bring to the boil and boil rapidly for 20 minutes, then drain and rinse again.

🍄 Meanwhile, put the tomatoes, onion, and garlic on a foil-lined baking tray under a preheated hot broiler. Broil, turning frequently, for 10-12 minutes, until charred all over.

🍄 Peel the onion and garlic, and cut the onion into chunks. Transfer to a food processor, add the tomatoes, and blend until smooth.

🍄 Heat the olive oil in a large skillet. Add the thyme, peppercorns, and coriander and cumin seeds, and fry for 30 seconds to flavor the oil. Stir in the purée and gently fry for a few minutes.

🍄 Add the drained beans and the broth. Bring to the boil, then simmer over medium heat for 30 minutes, until the beans are very soft.

🍄 Remove the thyme sprigs, then blend about half the beans in a food processor. Return this purée to the pan, add salt to taste, and reheat gently for 5-10 minutes.

🍄 Sprinkle with the coriander (cilantro) and top with avocado and chili. Serve with lime segments to squeeze over the soup.

Broccoli and Pine Nut Frittata
with Roasted Pepper Sauce

Also known as pine nuts, Indian nuts, pignolias, and piñones, pine kernels come mainly from the cones of the stone pine (Pinus pinea). Deliciously nutty with a sweet, delicate flavor, pine kernels have been part of the Mediterranean diet since the days of the Romans and are also a staple of the native American diet. They are an excellent source of magnesium, potassium, and vitamin E, and a good source of iron, zinc, and folate. According to Chinese medicine, they are a "warm" and sweet food which improves "cold" conditions and stimulates the flow of the life force *chi* and hence the blood circulation. Pine kernels are considered a yin tonic and, as such, will build up "the deepest reserves of subtle nourishment." In Ayurvedic medicine, pine kernels are considered sweet, heavy, and oily in quality, and are best eaten in small quantities.

• SERVES 4-6 •

Preparation time: 35 minutes
Cooking time: 1 hour
3 tablespoons pine kernels
2 cups broccoli flowerets
4 medium eggs
4 egg whites
6 tbsp shredded low-fat Swiss-style cheese
¼ teaspoon salt
freshly ground black pepper
1 teaspoon grapeseed or safflower oil
1 tablespoon butter

FOR THE SAUCE:

3 red bell peppers
2 tablespoons olive oil
1 small onion, minced
1 teaspoon minced fresh thyme
1 garlic clove, minced
1 tablespoon white wine vinegar
1 tablespoon tomato paste
1¼ cups vegetable broth
salt and freshly ground black pepper
1 tablespoon butter

TO SERVE:

salad of mixed leaves
warm French bread

To make the sauce, place the bell peppers in a roasting pan and roast in a preheated oven at 450° for 15-20 minutes, turning frequently, until the skin blackens and blisters. Allow the bell peppers to cool, then peel away the skin and remove the tops and seeds. Chop the flesh roughly and set aside.

Heat the olive oil in a saucepan and gently fry the onion with the thyme for about 5 minutes, until the onion is translucent. Add the garlic, and fry for another minute or two. Stir in the vinegar, tomato paste, broth, and salt and pepper. Simmer for 5 minutes.

Transfer the mixture to a food processor or blender and blend with the chopped peppers until smooth. Press through a fine sieve, then return the mixture to the pan. Bring to the boil, then simmer briskly for about 10 minutes, until thickened. Whisk in the butter. Set aside and keep warm while you make the frittata.

Toast the pine kernels in a preheated oven at 350° for about 3 minutes, until golden-brown in color.

Trim the broccoli flowerets where the head meats the stalk, reserving the stalks. Divide the heads into small pieces no more than 1 inch in diameter, and chop the stalks into small pieces.

Plunge the broccoli into a large pan of boiling salted water for 2 minutes, then drain thoroughly.

Beat together the whole eggs, egg whites, cheese, salt, and pepper until well mixed. Stir in the broccoli and pine kernels.

Heat the oil and butter in a 9½-10 inch nonstick skillet. Pour in the egg mixture, stirring so that the broccoli is evenly distributed. Cover, and cook over medium-low heat for about 10 minutes, until almost set.

Slide the frittata onto a large serving platter, cover with the skillet, then invert it back into the pan. Return to the heat to brown the other side. Slide the frittata onto the platter again and keep it warm.

Cut the frittata into wedges and serve with the sauce, a salad of mixed leaves, and warm bread.

Pumpkin
~ seeds ~

Highly nutritious, pumpkin seeds (pepitas) are rich in protein and an excellent source of magnesium, iron, zinc, and omega-3 fatty acids. They provide plenty of B vitamins too. Being rich in antioxidant nutrients, pumpkin seeds can be effective in the prevention of some cancers. Although not eaten in large quantities, a handful of seeds makes an energy-boosting snack and a nutritious addition to salads, soups, casseroles, and bakes. They can also be sprouted.

Natural medicine practitioners prescribe pumpkin seeds for a variety of ailments, particularly as a laxative and purgative. Pumpkin seeds are also a source of a richly flavored, golden-brown oil of the unsaturated kind, rich in vitamin E — delicious sprinkled over salads. It is not widely available, so if you come across a bottle, be sure to add it to your collection of healthy oils.

Warm Butternut Squash Salad

• SERVES 4 •

Preparation time: 25 minutes

Cooking time: 25 minutes

1 butternut squash weighing about 2 pounds

7-8 tablespoons olive oil

½ teaspoon black peppercorns, coarsely crushed

coarse sea salt

1 cup coarsely shredded young spinach

1 cup coarsely shredded green cabbage

1 small kohlrabi, cut into matchstick strips

3 tablespoons pumpkin seeds

1 tablespoon wine vinegar

2 tablespoons orange juice

pumpkin seed oil (optional)

chopped flat-leafed parsley or chives, to garnish

Tomato and Pumpkin Seed Bread to serve

Cut the squash in half crosswise at the point where the rounded part meets the neck. Cut the skin off each piece. Quarter the rounded part, and remove the seeds and fibers. Slice lengthwise into 1/4-inch thick segments. Cut the neck in half lengthwise, then crosswise into ¼-inch slices.

Heat the oil with the peppercorns in a large skillet over medium heat. Fry the squash in batches, turning carefully with tongs, until lightly browned. Sprinkle with sea salt. Remove to a colander set over a bowl and leave to drain.

Toss together the spinach, cabbage, kohlrabi, and 2 tablespoons of the pumpkin seeds, and arrange on individual serving plates.

Return any oil drained from the squash to the pan. Reheat, add the vinegar and orange juice, and allow to bubble for a few seconds.

Arrange the squash on top of the leafy vegetables, then pour over the pan juices. Drizzle with a little pumpkin seed oil, if using. Sprinkle with the remaining pumpkin seeds and herbs.

Tomato and Pumpkin Seed Bread

A delicious tomato-flavored bread — the perfect accompaniment to Warm Butternut Squash Salad.

• MAKES 2 LOAVES •

Preparation time: 45 minutes, plus proving

Cooking time: 45-50 minutes

6 cups unbleached all-purpose flour

1½ teaspoons salt

1½ teaspoons sugar

1 package active dry yeast

1 tablespoon pumpkin seed oil or olive oil

about 2 cups tepid water

7 tablespoons sun-dried tomato paste

6 tablespoons pumpkin seeds

flour for dusting

Sift the flour, salt, sugar, and yeast into a large warmed bowl. Make a well in the center and gradually stir in the oil and water, to form a soft dough. Knead on a well-floured work surface for at least 15 minutes, until smooth and springy.

Put the dough in a large, oiled bowl and cover with plastic wrap. Leave to stand in a warm place for 1-2 hours, until doubled in size.

Knock back the risen dough and spread the sun-dried tomato paste over it. Sprinkle with the pumpkin seeds. Roll up and knead until smooth. The tomato paste will make the dough rather sticky, but it will eventually become springy after kneading again.

Divide the dough in half and place in two greased and floured 6½ x 4-inch loaf pans. Dust with flour and leave to rise again in a warm place, until doubled in size.

Bake in a preheated oven at 400° for 45-50 minutes, spraying with water three times during the first 10 minutes of cooking for a crisp crust.

Eggplant, Artichoke, and Tomato Phyllo Tart

A crisp, richly-flavored tart that will have you coming back for more — it's worth making two. Phyllo or strudel dough contains one-tenth of the fat of ordinary shortcrust dough, therefore it is a healthier option for tarts, flans, and pies. Dab it very lightly with the chili oil.

• S E R V E S 4 - 6 •

Preparation time: 45 minutes

Cooking time: 40 minutes

5 tablespoons olive oil

½ teaspoon chili powder

four 13 x 13-inch sheets phyllo or strudel dough

1 eggplant weighing about 12 ounces, sliced into ¼-inch circles

3 oil-cured bottled or canned artichokes, quartered lengthwise

3 large garlic cloves, unpeeled

4 plum tomatoes

salt and freshly ground black pepper

2 ounces dry goat's cheese, crumbled

3 ounces mozzarella cheese, sliced

2 teaspoons chopped fresh thyme

a few basil leaves, torn

🐾 Combine the olive oil with the chili powder and use to brush the base and sides of a 1½-inch deep, 9-inch, loose-bottomed pie pan.

🐾 Cover the pastry with a clean, damp kitchen towel. Taking one sheet at a time, dab lightly on one side with the chili oil and lower into the pan, covering the base and pressing the pastry up the sides. Fold the edges over before adding the next sheet. Rotate each sheet so that the corners are offset. Bake in a preheated oven at 400° for 12-15 minutes, until pale golden in color.

🐾 Brush the eggplant slices on both sides with the chili oil and place on a baking tray with the artichokes and garlic cloves. Bake for 20 minutes at the same temperature as the phyllo pastry case, turning the eggplant and brushing with more oil if necessary. Remove the skins from the garlic and mash the flesh.

🐾 Meanwhile, cover the tomatoes with boiling water for 30 seconds. Slip off the skins and cut in half horizontally. Remove the seeds and core. Cut into thin circles, place on a double thickness of paper towel, and pat dry.

🐾 Lightly smear the pastry case with the garlic. Arrange the eggplant and tomato slices on top, alternating them in overlapping circles. Add the artichokes and season generously with salt and pepper. Top with the cheeses and sprinkle with the chopped thyme.

🐾 Bake the tart for 15-20 minutes, until the vegetables are heated through and the cheese has melted. Sprinkle with basil and serve at once.

Beneficial
Boosts

AFTERNOON SNACKS

On the whole, it's a good idea to avoid snacks between meals. Doing so gives the system time to completely digest the previous meal, and leaves you feeling properly hungry and ready for the next. However, blood sugar levels may fluctuate, often dropping to their lowest point in the afternoon, and as a result some people experience a real and urgent hunger — often to the point of weakness. In such cases, it is best to adopt a "little and often" policy, and to maintain energy levels with small, regular quantities of easily digested nutritious food.

Some people may feel in need of a snack not because they are physically in need of food but for deeper psychological reasons. They may be bored or unhappy, or have a difficult piece of work to do. All of these situations can create feelings of hunger that are hard to ignore.

Provided snacks are eaten in moderation, and they are nutritious, eating between meals should do little harm. A piece of fruit, chunks of raw vegetable, a handful of dried raisins, or even a glass of water can all help to stave off hunger pangs. If you need to eat snacks regularly, make sure you have a supply of healthy titbits prepared in advance and kept to hand. That way you won't be tempted to buy unhealthy manufactured snacks.

We have included recipes for some deeply satisfying cakes and muffins. There are also ideas for quickly made fruit shakes and whips. Served chilled, these are popular with children and make a refreshing snack on a hot summer afternoon.

Chocolate, Cranberry, and Walnut Muffins

Dried cranberries make delicious nuggets of tart sweetness in these easy-to-make, low-fat muffins. Treat yourself to a couple if you suffer from mid-afternoon energy dip.

• MAKES 12 •

Preparation time: 30 minutes
Cooking time: 25 minutes
¼ cup butter or non-hydrogenated margarine
⅓ cup unrefined light brown sugar
finely grated zest and juice of 1 orange
1 egg, beaten
2¼ cups whole-wheat flour
2 tablespoons unsweetened cocoa powder
1 tablespoon baking powder
1 teaspoon baking soda
¾ cup low-fat or 2% milk
½ cup dried cranberries
2 tablespoons chopped walnuts

🍄 Cream the butter or margarine, sugar, and orange zest together in a large bowl, until light and fluffy. Whisk the egg until frothy and add to the creamed mixture a little at a time, mixing well.
🍄 Combine the flour, cocoa powder, baking powder, and baking soda, and stir into the creamed mixture. Add the orange juice and milk, then stir in the dried cranberries and walnuts.
🍄 Spoon into greased muffin cups and bake in a preheated oven at 400° for 25 minutes, until well risen and firm to touch.

Lemon Rice Cake

• MAKES 12-16 SLICES •

Preparation time: 30 minutes
Cooking time: 2 hours 30 minutes
1 quart low-fat or 2% milk
pinch of salt
2 lemons
½ cup sugar
½ cup round-grain rice
4 eggs, separated, plus 1 yolk
2 tablespoons flaked almonds
2 tablespoons pine kernels
3 tablespoons finely chopped candied citrus peel
1 teaspoon vanilla extract
confectioner's sugar for dusting

🍄 Finely grate the rind of one lemon. Put the milk, salt, rind, and 3 tablespoons of the sugar in a saucepan and bring to the boil. Stir in the rice, then simmer over very low heat, uncovered, for 1½ hours. Stir the mixture occasionally with a wooden spoon to prevent sticking. Leave to cool.
🍄 Meanwhile, lightly grease and line an 8-inch square cake pan.
🍄 Beat the egg yolks and the remaining sugar in a large bowl. Add the rice mixture, nuts, candied peel, and vanilla extract, stirring well to blend.
🍄 Whisk the egg whites until stiff, and fold into the mixture.
🍄 Pour the mixture into the prepared pan, leveling the surface with a palette knife. Bake in a preheated oven at 350° for 1 hour. Leave to cool in the pan before turning out.
🍄 Peel the remaining lemon very thinly. Cut into very fine matchstick threads. Plunge into boiling water for 2-3 minutes, then drain.
🍄 When ready to serve, dust the cake with the confectioner's sugar, scatter with the lemon peel, and cut into small squares.

~ Sesame ~

Sesame (benne) has been cultivated in the orient for thousands of years and was used by the ancient Greeks, Egyptians, and Persians. It has a wide range of medical and pharmaceutical uses, as well as being invaluable in the kitchen. The seeds are a useful and tasty source of protein, and are rich in iron, calcium, magnesium, zinc, and vitamin E. They can be used in all sorts of dishes — salads, soups, stews, sauces, savory and sweet spreads, and baked foods. The seeds are very oily and produce an excellent cooking oil, high in mono- and polyunsaturated fatty acids. Medical herbalists use sesame seeds to treat constipation, hemorrhoids, and genito-urinary infections. In India, they are eaten as special warming food in cool, damp weather, and a decoction of the seeds is a remedy for delayed menstruation. In Chinese medicine, the seeds are considered to have demulcent, lubricating properties.

Olive Oil, Sesame, and Honey Cake

Full of exotic flavors, this unusual cake is adapted from a Middle Eastern recipe. It is made with olive oil, which is high in monounsaturates, instead of the more usual butter or margarine. The crunchy sesame topping gives a beautiful nutty flavor. Despite the light texture, the cake is very rich and a small piece will keep your energy levels high for hours to come.

• MAKES 12-16 SLICES •

Preparation time: 55 minutes

Cooking time: 1 hour 10 minutes

2 tablespoons dried sour cherries or cranberries

½ cup whole almonds with skin

1¼ cups cake flour

1¼ cups whole-wheat flour

2 teaspoons baking powder

3 tablespoons raisins

2 pinches saffron threads

2 tablespoons milk

4 eggs

¾ cup superfine sugar

1 cup extra-virgin olive oil

finely grated zest and juice of 1 large lemon

3 tablespoons sesame seeds

2 tablespoons honey

🐝 Preheat the oven to 350°. Grease and line an 8-inch square cake pan.

🐝 Put the cherries or cranberries in a small bowl and barely cover with boiling water. Leave to soak.

🐝 Spread the almonds on a baking tray and roast in the oven for 10 minutes. Chop roughly and leave to cool.

🐝 Sift together the flours and baking powder, returning to the bowl any bran sifted out from the whole-wheat flour. Mix the raisins and almonds with enough of the flour mixture to coat them. This will prevent them from sinking.

🐝 Put the saffron and milk in a small pan and heat very gently without boiling, until the milk is bright yellow. Alternatively, put them in a small glass or plastic bowl and heat in a microwave oven for a few seconds.

🐝 Beat the eggs and sugar for 5-7 minutes, until very pale and thick. Beat in alternate spoonfuls of olive oil and about half the flour. Then beat in the lemon zest and juice, and the saffron infusion.

🐝 Drain the cherries or cranberries, reserving the soaking liquid. Mix the cherries or cranberries with the raisins and almonds, adding another tablespoon of the flour. Fold the fruits and nuts into the egg mixture, mixing well, then fold in the remaining flour.

🐝 Pour the cake mixture into the prepared pan and sprinkle evenly with the sesame seeds. Bake on a medium-low shelf for 1 hour 10 minutes, resisting the temptation to open the oven door during the first 30 minutes. The cake is cooked when a skewer inserted into the center comes out clean. Allow to cool in the pan for 10 minutes.

🐝 Meanwhile, gently heat the honey and 4 tablespoons of the cherry or cranberry juice in a small pan. Remove the cake from the pan and pour the cherry or cranberry juice mixture over it.

~ Yogurt ~

The nutritional and medical properties of yogurt have been recognized in the Middle East and eastern Europe for centuries. Its health-promoting attributes were once thought to be the reason for the longevity of Bulgarian peasants. It is a useful source of calcium and phosphorus, and contains riboflavin (vitamin B2) and vitamin B12. Yogurt is a "live" food made by incubating a natural bacteria, lactobacilli, with pasteurised milk. Brands containing *Lactobacillus acidophilus* are the most therapeutic. Yogurt has been subjected to countless research studies and is now acknowledged as genuinely health-promoting. It is believed to boost the immune system and to discourage the proliferation of harmful bacteria and yeasts in the gut. It is helpful in treating *Candida albicans* and gastro-intestinal disorders, and also helps replace valuable intestinal bacteria destroyed by antibiotics.

Yogurt, Banana, and Dried Apricot Shake

Dried apricots and bananas are packed with energy-giving carbohydrates. Keep some apricot purée in the refrigerator ready for the blender.

• SERVES 1-2 •
Preparation time: 10 minutes
Cooking time: 5 minutes
¼ cup dried apricots, *preferably unsulfured*
1 *small banana*
⅔ *cup plain yogurt*
3 *tablespoons orange juice*
2-3 *tablespoons 2% or semi-skim milk*

TO DECORATE:
toasted flaked almonds
twist of orange

🍂 Put the apricots in a small saucepan with ¾ cup water. Bring to the boil and simmer for 5-7 minutes, until soft.

🍂 Tip the apricots into a food processor or blender with the cooking liquid, and purée until smooth. Leave the purée to cool in the blender goblet.

🍂 Slice the banana and add to the apricots with the yogurt and orange juice. Blend again, until smooth, thinning with a little milk if necessary. Pour into tumblers, sprinkle with the almonds, and decorate with a twist of orange.

Kiwifruit and Strawberry Pignolia

This vitamin- and mineral-packed slush makes a refreshing summer afternoon snack. It is a variation of strawberry pignolia — a dish popular among Seventh Day Adventists. They obviously appreciate the health-giving properties of pignoli (pine kernels — see page 32).

• SERVES 2-3 •
Preparation time: 15 minutes
Cooking time: 5 minutes
4 *tablespoons pine kernels*
8 *kiwifruits*
2 *small bananas, sliced*
1 *tablespoon clear honey such as acacia or orange blossom*
2 *tablespoons lime juice*
4 *tablespoons plain thickset yogurt*
4 *strawberries, sliced*

🍂 Put the pine kernels on a baking tray and toast them for 3-5 minutes in a preheated oven at 350°, until golden-brown. Take care not to let them burn. Leave to cool.

🍂 Peel the kiwifruits, chop the flesh roughly, and purée in a blender until smooth. Press through a fine sieve to remove the seeds. This is not strictly necessary, but they turn the dish an unappetizing shade of khaki.

🍂 Set aside a tablespoon of toasted pine kernels for decoration. Put the rest in a blender with the bananas, honey, and lime juice. Purée until smooth.

🍂 Combine the purée with the sieved kiwifruit and pour into serving bowls. Swirl in a spoonful of yogurt, and top with the sliced strawberries and reserved pine kernels.

Palate
Awakeners

APPETIZERS

Appetizers do exactly that — they get the tastebuds tingling and set the tone for the rest of the meal. They may be salads, soups, mousses, dips, pâtés, finger foods, little pastry parcels — the variations are endless, but appetizers should not be too complicated or overloaded with fat.

A well-chosen appetizer should be light and tasty, and complement the dish you plan to serve next; the serving should be small enough to leave people wanting more. Cold appetizers are probably the easiest since they can be prepared in advance — a good idea when your chosen entrée is time-consuming to make. An interesting, colorful salad is the simplest and one of the most nutritious choices, and will not detain you in the kitchen for too long.

When planning a meal, try and aim for variety in texture, flavor, color, and temperature — not only between courses, but within a course. Contrast cold with hot, raw with cooked, crisp with soft, acid with sweet. If you are an instinctive cook, you'll do this anyway. This way, your meals will be a joy to eat, and the nutritional balance is likely to be a healthy one.

In this chapter, you'll find a choice of salad-based appetizers which positively sing with color and flavor. Crunchy nuts and crisp lettuce are mixed with soft-textured fruits and vegetables, fiery spices are tamed with yogurt, and sizzling hot shrimp are served on cool leaves. Most can be prepared in under an hour, and all of them are low in fat and packed with vitamins and minerals.

HEALING FOOD

~ Broiled ~ and roasted vegetables

If you want to reduce the fat in your diet, oven-roasting or broiling vegetables is a delicious and nutritious way of preparing them. You will need hardly any oil — sometimes none at all, especially if you use a nonstick roasting pan. Because the vegetables are not immersed in cooking liquid, fewer nutrients are lost, although some will inevitably be destroyed by heat. Vegetables such as peppers, zucchini, red onions, and tomatoes are all good. Whole heads of garlic and fleshy chili peppers can be roasted too. This method greatly intensifies the flavors of these ingredients, and creates nutrient-rich juices that can be used to flavor dressings and sauces. This is a healthful way of cooking eggplant, since it normally soaks up tablespoons of oil when fried, but needs only the merest dab when roasted.

Roasted Eggplant and Peppers with Coriander Cream

• SERVES 4 •

Preparation time: 30 minutes
Cooking time: 20 minutes

1 large firm eggplant, thickly sliced crosswise
olive oil
salt and freshly ground black pepper
1 red and 1 yellow bell pepper, halved and seeded
1 small mild green chili pepper
4 tablespoons trimmed and chopped coriander
(cilantro)
3 tablespoons chopped flat-leafed parsley
2 green onions (scallions), chopped
1 garlic clove, crushed
2 tablespoons lime juice
1 teaspoon toasted cumin seeds
3 tablespoons heavy cream
⅓ cup thickset plain yogurt
½ Little Gem lettuce
coriander (cilantro) or parsley sprigs, to garnish

🐾 Preheat the oven to 475°. Brush the eggplant with oil and season. Arrange in a roasting pan with the bell and chili peppers. Roast for 10-20 minutes, until the eggplant is golden and the bell and chili peppers are blackened.

🐾 Remove the skins and seeds from the bell and chili peppers. Cut the bell peppers into large squares. Cut the eggplant slices in half.

🐾 Put the coriander (cilantro), parsley, green onions (scallions), and chili pepper in a blender with the garlic, lime juice, salt, pepper, and most of the cumin seeds. Blend for 3 minutes. Pour into a bowl and stir in the cream and yogurt.

🐾 Arrange the lettuce on serving plants with the eggplant and bell pepper on top. Add the coriander (cilantro) sauce, and sprinkle with a little olive oil and a few cumin seeds.

Papaya and Snow Pea Salad with Lime and Pistachio Dressing

A vitamin-packed, colorful salad with a tangy dressing. Like all orange-fleshed fruit, papaya is an excellent source of beta-carotene. It is also rich in enzymes that may aid digestion.

• SERVES 4 •

Preparation time: 30 minutes

1 cup trimmed snow peas
3 tablespoons shelled pistachio nuts
1 medium-large ripe papaya
lime juice
1 head butter lettuce or 2 heads Little Gem, leaves
separated, tough stalks removed
1 kiwifruit, peeled and thinly sliced crosswise
1 tablespoon chopped fresh mint

FOR THE DRESSING:
1 tablespoon lime juice
salt
freshly ground black pepper
3 tablespoons grapeseed oil
3 tablespoons walnut or almond oil

🐾 Plunge the snow peas into boiling water for 30 seconds. Drain immediately and leave to cool. Slice in half diagonally.

🐾 Cover the pistachios with boiling water. Leave for 5 minutes, drain, and slip off their skins.

🐾 Combine the dressing ingredients in a screw-top jar, and shake until smooth.

🐾 Cut the papaya in half, scoop out the seeds, and peel carefully. Cut crosswise into neat slices and sprinkle with lime juice.

🐾 Divide the lettuce between serving plates and arrange the papaya, kiwifruit, and snow peas attractively on top. Sprinkle with the nuts and mint, and spoon over enough dressing to coat.

~ Chickpeas ~

Chickpeas (garbanzo beans) and the flour made from them are a rich source of iron and folate, especially needed during pregnancy. Chickpeas are also a good source of protein, fiber, calcium, magnesium, potassium, and vitamin E. They are one of the easiest pulses to digest, and perhaps the most delicious to eat. The flour, which is easily obtainable from healthfood stores, makes tasty pancakes and fritters with a flavor that can only be described as warm and mellow. It contains no gluten, so is useful for those suffering from celiac disease. It is also a useful egg substitute — in place of each egg, use 1 tablespoon of chickpea flour mixed with enough cold water to form a paste. Oriental medicine classifies chickpeas as sweet and neutral in terms of yin and yang, and they are valued for their anti-inflammatory action, particularly on the urino-genital system.

Chickpea Crêpes with Black Bean, Carrot, and Mango Salad

• SERVES 6 •

Preparation time: 50 minutes

Cooking time: 30 minutes

FOR THE CREPES:

1⅓ cups chickpea (gram) flour

1 teaspoon salt

1 teaspoon black sesame seeds

½ teaspoon ground turmeric

freshly ground black pepper

1¼ cups water

peanut oil

FOR THE DRESSING:

1 tablespoon lime juice

1 tablespoon light olive oil

2 tablespoons macadamia oil or unrefined hazelnut oil

salt and freshly ground black pepper

FOR THE SALAD:

⅓ cup black turtle beans, soaked overnight

salt

3 carrots

4-inch piece cucumber

⅓ cup diced mango

2 tablespoons chopped coriander (cilantro) leaves

2 tablespoons macadamia or hazelnuts

½ teaspoon dark brown sugar

finely grated zest of 1 lime

To make the pancakes, sift the flour and salt into a bowl and combine with the sesame seeds, turmeric, and pepper. Make a well in the center and gradually whisk in the water, drawing in the flour from around the edge. Cover, and leave to stand while you make the dressing and salad.

To make the dressing, whisk all the ingredients together in a small bowl.

To make the salad, drain the beans and put them in a saucepan with fresh water to cover. Bring to the boil and boil rapidly for 15 minutes, then simmer briskly for another 10 minutes, until tender. Add salt to taste during the last five minutes of cooking time. Drain and leave to cool.

Peel the carrots and cut into 2-inch chunks. Using a swivel peeler, shave the chunks into wafers, discarding the woody core.

Peel the cucumber and halve lengthwise. Scoop out the seeds and thinly slice the flesh diagonally.

Combine the carrots, beans, mango, and coriander (cilantro) in a bowl. Pour the dressing over the salad, tossing well. Leave to stand at room temperature.

Put the nuts in a small roasting pan and roast in a preheated oven at 350° for 10-12 minutes, until golden-brown. If the nuts have skins, rub them off with a clean, dry kitchen towel. Chop the nuts and mix with the sugar, half a teaspoon of salt, and the lime zest.

To cook the pancakes, whisk the batter again. Heat 2 teaspoons of peanut oil in a heavy-based, 9-inch nonstick skillet or crêpe pan, until almost smoking. Swirl in 4 tablespoons of the mixture with a circular motion to make a very thin, 6-inch circle. Lift the edges when just set and let the uncooked mixture run underneath. Fry over a high heat for about 50 seconds on each side, until golden-brown. Repeat with the rest of the batter to make six pancakes, adding a little more oil as necessary. Leave the pancakes to cool on a rack.

To serve, put a mound of salad on top of each pancake. Sprinkle with the nut mixture.

Pecan Rice, Radish, and Radicchio with Griddled Shrimp

• SERVES 4 •

Preparation time: 35 minutes, plus marinating

Cooking time: 45 minutes

1 pound 7 ounces large raw shrimp, with shells

juice of 3-4 limes

1 small chili pepper, seeded and finely chopped

2 garlic cloves, minced

salt

olive oil

¾ cup cooked pecan, red, or wild rice

1 teaspoon sesame oil

½ teaspoon tamari (Japanese soy sauce)

1 tablespoon chopped coriander (cilantro) leaves

10-12 baby radishes, trimmed and sliced diagonally

8 radicchio leaves

3 green onions (scallions), shredded

4 tablespoons mung beansprouts

With the backs uppermost, cut nearly all the way through the shrimp shells and flesh. Turn over, open the shrimp out, and press flat. Put in a shallow dish. Sprinkle with 4 tablespoons of lime juice, chili pepper, garlic, salt, and enough oil to coat. Marinate for 1 hour. Toss the rice with the sesame oil, tamari, coriander (cilantro), a squeeze of lime and 1 tablespoon of olive oil. Season to taste. Mix in the radishes.

Divide the radicchio leaves between four serving dishes and pile the rice on top. Scatter with the green onion (scallion) shreds and the beansprouts.

Put the shrimp, shell side downward, on a hot griddle. Cook for 2-3 minutes, until just the center is still translucent. Turn them over and briefly cook on the other side, until opaque.

Arrange the shrimp on top of the rice salad and serve immediately.

Pink Grapefruit, Avocado, and Walnuts with Mixed Leaves

A light and refreshing salad of contrasting textures and flavors. Pink or red-fleshed grapefruit are slightly higher in vitamin C content compared with the yellow-fleshed varieties.

• SERVES 4 •

Preparation time: 15 minutes

1 large red-fleshed grapefruit

1 large avocado

lemon juice

2 ounces baby spinach leaves, coarsely shredded

3-4 handfuls frisée lettuce, torn into bite-sized pieces

small handful of watercress, land cress or chia

4 radishes, sliced diagonally

3 tablespoons walnut halves

extra-virgin olive oil

salt and freshly ground black pepper

walnut oil

Using a very sharp knife, cut a horizontal slice from the top and the bottom of the grapefruit. Remove the remaining peel and white parts by cutting downward following the contours of the fruit. Working over a bowl, cut down between the flesh and membrane of each segment. Ease out the flesh and put it in a bowl. Cut the segments in half crosswise and set aside with the juice.

Cut the avocado in half lengthwise then slice crosswise. Sprinkle with lemon juice.

Toss the salad greens with a few drops of olive oil — just enough to barely coat the leaves. Season with salt and freshly ground black pepper. Arrange on individual plates. Scatter with the radishes and walnut halves. Add the avocado and grapefruit segments. Sprinkle with the grapefruit juice and just a little dash of the walnut oil, and serve at once.

Kind
Cuisine

VEGETARIAN MAIN MEALS

Modern vegetarian cooking is colorful, tasty, and exciting. Even if you are not a vegetarian, a meat-free meal two or three times a week can bring new enjoyment to eating, and is likely to make you feel refreshed.

Vegetables, grains, nuts, pasta, beans, lentils, and sea vegetables supply all the nutrients needed for vibrant good health. These foods are naturally high in fiber, vitamins, and minerals, low in fat and supply adequate protein, especially if you combine them with small amounts of low-fat dairy products.

As well as providing sustenance and fulfilling nutritional requirements, a meal should engage all the senses. This is particularly important if you are cooking for people new to vegetarian food. A well-prepared meal delights the eye and sets the tastebuds working. This in turn produces the gastric juices necessary for effective digestion of food.

When planning a vegetarian meal, the emphasis can shift from the conventional format of a main dish with accompaniments; the dishes can have equal weight as they do in an Indian and Chinese menu.

The recipes in this chapter are inspired by the cooking of Japan, the Middle East, and Italy — cuisines based on sound nutritional principles. Although you may not have used some of the ingredients before, you should have no difficulty in finding them. With luck, you will discover a whole range of exciting new tastes and flavors that you will continue to use to good effect in other dishes.

HEALING FOOD

~ Wild rice ~

This is not a true rice, but the seeds of a North American wild aquatic grass. It has been a vital part of the culture of the Native Americans of the Minnesota area for thousands of years. Their name for it is "manoomin', meaning "good berry" or "good seed." The rice harvest is an annual ceremony at which prayers are offered to the Great Spirit, thanking him for the gift of this staple food. Weight for weight, wild rice contains twice the protein of white or brown rice, as well as more phosphorus, zinc, and riboflavin. Because of the higher protein content, wild rice is considered a warming food in Ayurvedic medicine, whereas rice is normally thought of as a "cold" food. In oriental medicine, it is considered a fortifying food for cold climates, and is believed to concentrate warmth in the lower body.

Red Cabbage Roulades *with Wild Rice and Nut Stuffing*

Red cabbage makes a change from green in these delicious nut-stuffed rolls.

• SERVES 4-6 •

Preparation time: 40 minutes

Cooking time: 1 hour 40 minutes

¼ wild rice

salt

bay leaf

2 red cabbages

4 tablespoons olive oil

2 tablespoons butter

3 tablespoons chopped mixed nuts

¼ cup minced onion

3 tablespoons chestnut mushrooms, minced

3 garlic cloves, minced

1 tablespoon chopped fresh marjoram, thyme, or rosemary

finely grated zest of 1 lemon

freshly ground black pepper

1 cup vegetable broth

chopped fresh thyme, to garnish

Roasted Red Pepper Sauce (page 32), to serve

Put the rice in a saucepan with ½ teaspoon of salt, the bay leaf, and enough water to cover by the depth of your thumbnail. Bring to the boil, then cover and simmer over very low heat for 30 minutes, until tender but still with some bite. Discard the bay leaf and put the rice into a bowl.

Cut off 1½ inches from the base of the cabbages and carefully peel away 12 outer leaves. Plunge the leaves into boiling water for 2-3 minutes. Rinse under cold running water and pat dry with paper towels. Using a small sharp knife, shave away the base of the stalk so that the leaves are easier to bend.

Cut away a lengthways segment from one of the cabbages and finely shred about 2½ ounces, discarding the tough center.

To make the stuffing, heat 1 tablespoon of the oil and half the butter in a large frying pan. Fry the nuts for 3-4 minutes, until golden-brown. Add to the cooked rice and wipe out the pan.

Heat the remaining oil and most of the remaining butter, and gently fry the onion until translucent. Add the mushrooms and shredded cabbage, and fry over medium heat for 5 minutes. Stir in the garlic and herbs, and fry for another 2 minutes. Add to the nuts and rice.

Stir in the lemon zest, black pepper, salt to taste, and 6 tablespoons of the broth.

Divide the stuffing between the leaves, placing it at the stalk end. Fold over the bottom, then the sides of each leaf and roll up. Place seam side down in a single layer in a shallow greased baking dish, packing them tightly. Pour in the remaining broth and dot with butter.

Cover the dish with a double thickness of foil. Bake for 45-55 minutes in a preheated oven at 350°, until the cabbage is tender.

~ Sea ~ vegetables

Sea vegetables, or seaweed, have been used as food, medicine, and fertilizer for thousands of years. Earliest records of their use date back to 6 BC in China. They are high in fiber, low in fat, and rich in iodine, B vitamins, and antioxidants C and E. Iodine helps prevent goitre (swelling of the thyroid gland in the neck) — a disease virtually unknown in Japan, where sea vegetables have long been part of the diet. In oriental medicine, they are highly valued for their healing properties which include clearing phlegm, soothing the digestive tract, general detoxification, alleviating bloating and water retention, and reducing blood cholesterol levels. They are also thought to promote healthy hair and to prevent its loss. Sea vegetables have one drawback — their high sodium content makes them unsuitable for anyone on a low-sodium diet.

Sea Vegetable and Shiitake Stir-Fry with Brown Rice

Hiziki is one of the milder sea vegetables, and a good one to try if you're new to them.

• SERVES 4 •
Preparation time: 25 minutes
Cooking time: 10 minutes
¼ cup dried hiziki
2 tablespoons tamari (Japanese soy sauce) or shoyu
1 tablespoon rice vinegar
1 teaspoon wasabi powder (optional)
2 tablespoons safflower or grapeseed oil
2 teaspoons toasted sesame oil
3 garlic cloves, finely chopped
1-inch piece fresh ginger root, finely chopped
1 yellow bell pepper, cut into matchsticks
½ cup shiitake mushrooms, thinly sliced
1¾ cups cooked brown rice
4 green onions (scallions), green parts included, cut into matchstick shreds

🐾 Rinse the hiziki and soak in cold water for at least 1 hour. Drain, reserving the soaking liquid.
🐾 Combine the tamari and rice vinegar, and stir in the wasabi powder, if using.
🐾 Heat the oils in a wok or large skillet until almost smoking. Throw in the garlic and ginger, and sizzle for a few seconds. Then add the bell pepper, mushrooms, hiziki, and 2 tablespoons of the soaking liquid. Stir-fry for 2 minutes, then tip into a bowl and keep warm.
🐾 Add the rice to the wok, sprinkle with 3 tablespoons of the hiziki liquid, and stir-fry for 2-3 minutes. Stir in the tamari mixture.
🐾 Return the vegetables to the pan with the green onions (scallions) and stir thoroughly until heated through.

Sea Vegetable, Carrot, and Snow Peas with Rice Noodles

Arame is a mildly flavored sea vegetable sold in healthfood stores and Japanese food stores.

• SERVES 4 •
Preparation time: 20 minutes, plus soaking
Cooking time: 35 minutes
¼ cup dried arame
2 tablespoons peanut oil
1 tablespoon mirin
1 tablespoon tamari (Japanese soy sauce) or shoyu
⅔ cup flat cellophane noodles
1 teaspoon toasted sesame oil
2 carrots, cut into matchsticks
½ cup leek, cut into shreds
¼ cup snow peas, cut into thin diagonal slices
2 tablespoons trimmed watercress, chopped

🐾 Rinse the arame and put in a bowl with enough water to cover. Leave to soak for 15 minutes, then drain, reserving the soaking liquid.
🐾 Heat 2 tablespoons of peanut oil in a large skillet. Add the arame and stir-fry over medium heat for 1-2 minutes. Add the mirin, tamari and 1 cup of the soaking water. Bring to the boil, then cover and simmer over gentle heat for 25 minutes, until the liquid has reduced by half.
🐾 Meanwhile, cook the noodles according to the package instructions. Drain, toss with the toasted sesame oil, and transfer to a warmed serving dish.
🐾 Add the carrot and leek to the arame. Cover and cook again for 5 minutes, adding a little more soaking water if necessary.
🐾 Add the snow peas and watercress. Cover and cook for another 30 seconds. Check the seasoning, and add more tamari if necessary. Pour the arame mixture over the noodles.

Asian Ratatouille with Gingered Rice

This Mediterranean-style vegetable stew is given an oriental twist with some warming ginger, soy sauce, and sesame seeds.

• SERVES 6 •

Preparation time: 35 minutes

Cooking time: 45 minutes

5 tablespoons light olive oil

1 small red onion, cut into ¾-inch squares

2 garlic cloves, minced

1-inch piece fresh root ginger, minced

1 pound (3 cups) plum tomatoes, peeled, seeded, and chopped

2 tablespoons tamari (Japanese soy sauce) or shoyu

1½ tablespoons rice wine

1 teaspoon sugar

salt and freshly ground black pepper

1 fresh green chili pepper, seeded and chopped

2 teaspoons coriander seeds, crushed

1 small eggplant, cut into ¾-inch chunks

⅔ cup (5 ounces) sliced shiitake mushrooms

2 small zucchini, sliced diagonally

1 red bell pepper, seeded and cut into chunks

2 teaspoons sesame seeds, toasted

FOR THE RICE:

3 tablespoons groundnut oil

1-2 teaspoons hot chili oil

2 garlic cloves, minced

1-inch piece fresh root ginger, minced

1½ cups medium-grain white rice

1½ cups light vegetable broth

1¼ cups water

salt

2 tablespoons fresh lime or lemon juice

4 green onions (scallions), minced

2 tablespoons minced fresh coriander (cilantro)

🍄 Heat 1 tablespoon of the oil in a saucepan. Gently fry the onion for 5 minutes, until just soft. Add the garlic and ginger, and fry for 1 minute. Stir in the tomatoes, tamari, rice wine, and sugar. Season with salt and black pepper. Simmer over a very low heat for 15-20 minutes, stirring occasionally, until reduced and thickened.

🍄 Meanwhile, prepare the rice. Heat the oils in a skillet with a lid. Add the garlic and ginger, and fry for one minute. Add the rice and cook for 3-4 minutes, stirring, until all the grains are coated with oil. Pour in the broth, water, and a little salt. Bring to the boil, then cover tightly and simmer over very low heat for 15-20 minutes, until all the liquid has been absorbed. Remove from the heat and stir in the juice. Leave to stand, covered, for 10 minutes.

🍄 Meanwhile, heat the remaining olive oil in a large skillet until very hot. Add the chili pepper and coriander seeds, and sizzle for 30 seconds. Add the eggplant and shiitake mushrooms, and stir-fry over medium heat for 5 minutes. Stir in the remaining vegetables, and fry for 3 more minutes.

🍄 When the vegetables are just soft, pour in the tomato sauce, cover, and simmer for 10 minutes. Check the seasoning, and stir in the sesame seeds.

🍄 Stir the green onions (scallions) and coriander (cilantro) into the rice, and serve with the vegetables.

Black Bean, Squash, and Root Vegetable Casserole

• SERVES 6 •

Preparation time: 25 minutes, plus soaking

Cooking time: 1 hour 20 minutes

2 cups cooked black turtle beans

1 teaspoon cumin seeds

2 teaspoons coriander seeds

1 tablespoon sesame seeds

2 teaspoons dried oregano

2 tablespoons olive oil

1 onion, chopped

3 garlic cloves, crushed

1-2 fresh red chili peppers, seeded and chopped

1 butternut squash or small pumpkin, weighing about 1¼ pounds, peeled and cut into chunks

1 yellow yam or sweet potato, peeled and cut into chunks

2 large carrots, thickly sliced

2 potatoes, peeled and cut into chunks

1 celery root, weighing about 1 pound, peeled and cut into chunks

3 ounces frozen sweetcorn kernels

14-ounce can chopped tomatoes

1½ cups vegetable broth

salt and freshly ground black pepper

4 tablespoons chopped fresh coriander (cilantro)

2 tablespoons lime juice

🐾 Heat the seeds in a small skillet for 1-2 minutes. Add the oregano and heat for a few more seconds. Remove and crush.

🐾 Heat the oil in a casserole and fry the onion until translucent. Add the garlic and chili peppers, and fry for 2-3 minutes.

🐾 Add the seeds and the remaining ingredients, except the coriander (cilantro) and lime juice. Bring to the boil, cover, and simmer for 45 minutes. Add the herb and juice before serving.

Greens and Beans with Pasta and Garlic Chives

• SERVES 4-6 •

Preparation time: 25 minutes

Cooking time: 20 minutes

1 cup shelled young lima beans, fresh or frozen

9 ounces trimmed mixed large-leaf greens such as Swiss chard (silverbeet), collard greens, and spinach

3 tablespoons olive oil

1 white onion, minced

3 garlic cloves, minced

½ teaspoon dried jalapeño pepper flakes

½-⅔ cup vegetable broth

salt and freshly ground black pepper

finely grated zest of 1 lemon

3 tablespoons snipped garlic chives

1⅓ cups (10½ ounces) farfalle (bowtie noodles)

2 tablespoons butter

2 teaspoons finely chopped savory

parmesan shavings, to garnish

🐾 Plunge the lima beans into boiling water for 2 minutes. Rinse under cold running water, then slip off the skins.

🐾 Slice the leaves crosswise into ribbons.

🐾 Heat the oil in a large sauté pan with a lid. Add the onion and fry for 5 minutes. Add the pepper flakes and all but 1 teaspoon of the garlic, and fry until the garlic is just colored.

🐾 Stir in the greens and the broth, and season. Cover and cook over medium-low heat for 7-10 minutes. Stir in the lemon zest and 2 tablespoons of the chives.

🐾 Meanwhile, cook the pasta in boiling salted water until al dente. Drain, toss with the greens, and season.

🐾 Melt the butter and gently fry the remaining herbs for 1 minute. Stir in the beans, season, and heat through. Pour over the greens.

The Fruits of the Sea

FISH AND SEAFOOD ENTRÉES

The astonishing variety of fish and seafood is an unending source of delight to cook and diner alike. From the robust richness of tuna and the delicate flesh of snapper, to the salty tang of mussels steaming in a fragrant broth, the possibilities are endless.

Fish and seafood are as healthy as they are delicious. Weight for weight, they contain a healthier package of nutrients than meat and are not accompanied by the risks associated with saturated fats, as in meat. Indeed, their oils are positively beneficial to health, containing essential fatty acids strongly implicated in reducing the risk of heart disease and a host of other common diseases.

The inherent goodness and flavor of fish and seafood does away with complicated techniques. In many cases, simply broiling, steaming, or searing is all that's required. Being naturally tender, fish and seafood need only the briefest cooking time. In fact, fish and seafood are perfect convenience foods, particularly when you're tired or busy. It goes without saying that only perfectly fresh, top-quality specimens will do.

The recipes in this chapter draw on Pacific, Oriental, and Mediterranean cuisines, in which fish plays such an important part. You'll find ideas for zesty sauces to complement the richness of oily fish, as well as more subtle flavorings for delicate white fish. All are designed to enhance the natural, fresh flavors of the fish and seafood.

~ Seafood ~

Seafood is rich in protein and very low in unsaturated fats. Shellfish is rich in chromium, copper, and selenium, and seafood is rich in fluoride and iodine. It is the omega-3 fatty acids in seafood that make them healthy, with the potential to help lower blood cholesterol. While the cholesterol content of seafood is considered high, what is more important in controlling blood cholesterol is the amount of saturated fat in the diet. Seafood is low in saturated fat and high in omega-3 fatty acids. Fish has long been called "brain food" because of the relationship between low-fat protein in seafood and its impact on the neurotransmitters in the brain. Additionally, there is some agreement among the experts that protein (as in seafood) can counteract a "heavy" feeling induced by too much carbohydrate and add to alertness.

Mixed Seafood Rice

A spectacular and easily made dish for relaxed entertaining. Vary the seafood if you like — try adding crabmeat or clams. You will need about 1¾ pounds of seafood in total. Serve with a green salad and plenty of crusty bread.

• SERVES 6 •
Preparation time: 45 minutes
Cooking time: 50 minutes
3 tablespoons olive oil
1 onion, minced
2 garlic cloves, minced
1 red or yellow bell pepper, seeded and finely chopped
6 plum tomatoes, peeled, seeded, and diced
1 teaspoon paprika
2 bay leaves
salt and freshly ground black pepper
1¼ cups long-grain white rice
2½ cups hot fish or chicken broth
8 ounces monkfish, cut into chunks
6 large peeled raw shrimp
4 ounces sliced squid
1½ cups mussels, shells scrubbed clean
3 green onions (scallions), green parts included, chopped
lime wedges, to garnish

Heat the oil in a large skillet. Gently fry the onion for 5 minutes until translucent. Add the garlic and pepper, and fry until the garlic is just colored. Stir in the tomatoes, paprika, bay leaves, salt, and pepper. Gently fry for another 2-3 minutes.

Add the rice, stirring until translucent, then pour in the broth, and bring to the boil. Reduce the heat, cover, and simmer over low heat for 10 minutes without stirring.

Place the monkfish, shrimp, squid, and mussels on top of the rice. Cover and cook for another 15 minutes. Discard any mussels that have not opened, then continue to cook for 5-10 minutes more, until all the liquid has been absorbed.

Remove from the heat and scatter with the green onions (scallions). Leave to stand, covered, for 5 minutes. Garnish with the lime wedges immediately before serving.

~ Asian ~ greens

You can buy oriental greens in oriental food stores and good supermarkets. Bok Choy has thick, crisp, white stems and bright green leaves. Choy sum has grooved, white stems bearing tasty small yellow flowers. Tatsoi has dark green, rosette-like leaves, and mizuna has long, feathery, jagged leaves. If you have trouble finding them, use Chinese (Napa) cabbage, chia, cress, collard greens, mustard greens, or any other greenery you have to hand. Asian greens are vivid and emphatic — peppery, astringent, sometimes slightly bitter — and combine well with the richness of tuna. They are a powerhouse of vitamins and minerals including calcium, potassium, iron, and beta-carotene. They also contain "new"' antioxidants such as lutein and zeaxanthin, which some nutritionists believe to be as important as beta-carotene in cancer prevention.

Seared Tuna with Asian Greens

• SERVES 4 •

Preparation time: 20 minutes

Cooking time: 15 minutes

4 tuna steaks, weighing about 6 ounces each

light olive oil, for brushing

juice of ½ lime

freshly ground black pepper

1¾ pounds oriental greens such as bok choy, choy sum, mizuna, tatsoi, and mustard greens

6 tablespoons light chicken or vegetable broth

1½ tablespoons shoyu

2 tablespoons peanut oil

3 garlic cloves, finely sliced

2 thin slices fresh ginger root, minced

1 shallot, minced

salt

lime wedges and coriander (cilantro) sprigs, to garnish

Brush the tuna steaks with oil, sprinkle with lime juice, and season with pepper.

Trim the greens, rinse, and thoroughly pat dry. Slice any meaty stems into chunks. Combine the broth and shoyu.

Place the fish over hot coals on a barbecue or on a ridged cast-iron broiler pan, and broil for about 4 minutes each side, until charred on the outside but still pink inside.

Heat the peanut oil in a wok until almost smoking, swirling to coat the wok. Add the garlic, ginger, and shallot, and stir until the garlic is lightly colored. Add the greens and stir for 2-3 minutes, until just wilted. Pour in the broth and cook for another minute. Season with salt.

Lift the greens from the pan with a slotted spoon, and divide them between warmed plates. Place a tuna steak on top and garnish with a lime wedge and coriander (cilantro) sprig.

Oriental Steamed Snapper

• SERVES 4 •

Preparation time: 30 minutes, plus marinating

Cooking time: 40 minutes

1 whole red snapper (about 2¾ pounds) or bream, cleaned and gutted

1 teaspoon salt

2 teaspoons toasted sesame oil

6 green onions (scallions), cut into shreds

1-inch piece fresh ginger root, cut into shreds

2 garlic cloves, finely sliced

3 tablespoons shoyu

juice and finely grated zest of ½ lemon

2 tablespoons rice wine or dry sherry

½ teaspoon sugar

2 tablespoons peanut oil

freshly ground black pepper

thinly sliced lime, to garnish

plainly boiled rice, to serve

Line a roasting pan with lightly greased foil.

Score both sides of the fish with diagonal slashes. Rub the inside and outside of the fish with salt and sesame oil.

Scatter half the green onions (scallions) and ginger, and all the garlic over the foil. Place the fish on top.

Combine 2 tablespoons of the shoyu with the lemon juice and zest, rice wine, and sugar, and spoon over the fish. Parcel up loosely and leave for 30 minutes.

Bake in a preheated oven at 350° for 30-40 minutes, until just cooked. Lift the fish onto a warmed serving platter. Sprinkle with the remaining green onions (scallions) and ginger, and season with pepper.

Heat the peanut oil in a small saucepan until smoke rises. Pour it over the fish, and sprinkle with the remaining shoyu.

~ Oily fish ~

There is growing evidence that oil-rich fish such as salmon, mackerel, trout, herring, tuna, and sardines, may help prevent heart disease, high blood pressure, and rheumatic conditions. This is because such fish are a unique source of omega-3 fatty acids. Our bodies cannot manufacture these fatty acids, yet they play an essential role in our metabolism. They have been shown to discourage blood from clotting, which may help reduce the risk of heart attacks, strokes, and circulatory problems, as well as thin the blood naturally. They can also lower blood cholesterol levels. There are also indications that omega-3 fatty acids may help to improve certain skin conditions such as psoriasis. To gain significant health benefits, we should try and eat oil-rich fish at least twice a week.

Trout Fillets with Passion Fruit Sauce

Trout is an excellent source of vitamin D and contains a useful amount of selenium, a valuable trace mineral thought to help prevent cancer.

• S E R V E S   4 •

Preparation time: 15 minutes

Cooking time: 15 minutes

6 passion fruits (granadillas)

3 tablespoons very finely chopped fennel

2 tablespoons fresh orange juice

½ teaspoon sugar

4 tablespoons thickset yogurt

1 tablespoon butter

salt

4 trout fillets, weighing about 6 ounces each

light olive oil, for brushing

freshly ground black pepper

fennel fronds, to garnish

Cut the passion fruits (granadillas) in half and scoop out the pulp. Press through a sieve, reserving 1 tablespoon of the seeds.

Combine the sieved pulp, fennel, orange juice, and sugar in a small heavy-based saucepan. Cook over medium heat for about 3-5 minutes, until reduced by half. Remove from the heat and whisk in the yogurt and the reserved seeds. Return to the heat without allowing the sauce to boil. Whisk in the butter a little at a time. Season with salt and keep warm.

Brush the fish with oil and season it. Place the fish, skin side upward, under a very hot broiler and broil for 7-10 minutes, depending on the thickness of the fillets. Whisk the juices into the sauce.

Fish Kabobs with Coconut and Coriander Sauce

• S E R V E S   4 •

Preparation time: 30 minutes, plus marinating

Cooking time: 10 minutes

juice of 3-4 limes

1 tablespoon olive oil

2 large garlic cloves, crushed

½ teaspoon dried jalapeño chili flakes

freshly ground black pepper

14 ounces mackerel fillets, cut crosswise into 1-inch strips

14 ounces monkfish, cut into 1-inch chunks

16 kaffir lime leaves or bay leaves

F O R   T H E   S A U C E :

2 tablespoons roughly chopped fresh coriander (cilantro)

¼ cup coconut cream, crumbled

6 tablespoons low-fat plain yogurt

½-inch piece fresh ginger root, minced

1 garlic clove, chopped

finely grated zest and juice of 1 lime

¼-½ teaspoon jalapeño chili flakes

salt

Combine the lime juice, oil, garlic, chili flakes, and pepper in a shallow dish. Add the fish, stirring to coat, and leave for 1 hour.

Put all the sauce ingredients in a blender, and blend on high for 2 minutes, until smooth. Pour into a serving bowl and leave to stand at room temperature.

Thread the fish and lime or bay leaves onto 8 skewers. Place on a rack under a preheated very hot broiler or over hot coals, and cook for about 10 minutes, turning occasionally.

Serve with the sauce and rice or other whole grains, mixed with chopped fresh herbs.

Meat
Meals

MEAT, POULTRY, AND GAME ENTRÉES

Cooked and chosen with care, it is possible for meals based on lean meat, poultry, and game to contribute to a healthy diet, particularly if you exercise vigorously or are involved in heavy manual work. However, it is important to eat these foods in moderate amounts — especially red meat — taking into account the amount of fat, protein, and other nutrients present in the rest of the meal and the day's eating plan. If you eat a meat-based entrée in the evening, try and eat early enough for your system to be finished with the process of digestion before you go to bed. Best of all, reserve meat for savoring over a relaxed weekend or for a vacation lunch, with family and friends.

Eating is, after all, about enjoyment, not just sound nutritional principles. So if you like meat and poultry, let the succulent flavors and textures be a positive source of lip-smacking satisfaction. Your enjoyment will be even greater if you take the trouble to find a supplier whose stock is organically reared in humane surroundings. The flesh has more flavor, it is likely to be less fatty, and you won't be troubled by thoughts of residues from the hormones and antibiotics used for intensively reared stock. Game is usually free of such problems.

In the recipes that follow, you'll notice that the quantity of meat per serving is kept deliberately small. In most cases, it is part of a stir-fry or casserole where the bulk of the dish is made up of plenty of vegetables and beans or lentils. This is the healthiest way to serve meat.

Broiled Peppered Chicken with Thyme-Lime Pesto

Contrary to popular belief, most of the fat in chicken is unsaturated and will not raise blood cholesterol levels. However, the skin does contain some saturated fat. Choose a young, free-range bird that has been reared on corn rather than hormone- and antibiotic-laden feed.

• S E R V E S   4 •

Preparation time: 30 minutes, plus marinating

Cooking time: 50 minutes

1 *chicken weighing about 3 pounds*

1½ *tablespoons black peppercorns*

½ *tablespoon finely chopped fresh rosemary*

½ *tablespoon chopped fresh thyme*

2 *tablespoons lime juice*

1 *tablespoon olive oil*

sea salt

lime wedges and rosemary sprigs, to garnish

F O R   T H E   T H Y M E - L I M E   P E S T O :

2 *tablespoons fresh thyme leaves,*

preferably lemon thyme

4 *tablespoons minced flat-leafed parsley*

2 *garlic cloves, crushed*

2 *teaspoons finely grated lime rind*

1 *tablespoon lime juice*

salt and freshly ground black pepper

1½ *ounces shelled pistachio nuts*

⅓ *cup olive oil*

🌿 Place the chicken on a board, breast side downward. Cut off the wing tips and legs. Using kitchen scissors, cut along the entire length of the chicken either side of the backbone. Turn the chicken over and flatten the breastbone by pressing firmly with the heel of your hand. Put in a shallow dish.

🌿 Coarsely crush the peppercorns with the rosemary and thyme, using a pestle and mortar. Rub the mixture over the chicken, pressing it well into the flesh.

🌿 Whisk the lime juice and oil. Pour this over the chicken, patting into the flesh. Cover and put in the refrigerator to marinate for at least 2 hours or overnight, turning occasionally.

🌿 To make the pesto, pound the first 7 ingredients with a pestle and mortar. Scrape into a blender. With the motor running, gradually add olive oil, until the sauce emulsifies and thickens.

🌿 Allow the chicken to come to room temperature before cooking. Thread a skewer across both folded legs and another through the wings and breast and out the other side.

🌿 Preheat the broiler until very hot. Place the chicken skin side upward in a broiler pan without a rack. Sprinkle with salt. Position the pan approximately 6 inches from the heat source and broil for 15 minutes, until the skin is golden-brown.

🌿 Baste with the juices and turn the chicken over. Broil for another 20 minutes, then turn again, and broil for a final 15 minutes, until the juices run clear when the thickest part of the thigh is pierced with a skewer.

🌿 Cut into serving-size pieces and arrange in a warmed serving dish. Garnish and serve with the thyme-lime pesto.

Spiced Lamb and Apricot Kabobs

It is worth grinding your own spices rather than using commercial curry powder to make this flavorful marinade. Lamb and apricots are a classic combination in Middle Eastern cooking.

• SERVES 4 •

Preparation time: 40 minutes, plus marinating
Cooking time: 35 minutes

1 *pound boneless lean lamb, cut into 1-inch chunks*
⅔ *cup no-soak dried apricots, halved if they are large*
8 *pearl onions, halved*
8 *fresh bay leaves*
oil for brushing
2 *tablespoons chopped flat-leafed parsley*
saffron rice and a mixed leaf salad, to serve

FOR THE MARINADE:

2 *teaspoons fennel seeds*
½ *teaspoon cumin seeds*
seeds from 4 cardamom pods
½ *teaspoon ground turmeric*
¼ *teaspoon cayenne pepper*
½ *teaspoon garam masala*
¾-*inch piece fresh ginger root*
3 *tablespoons olive oil*
2 *onions, minced*
3 *garlic cloves, minced*
1 *tablespoon dark brown sugar*
½ *teaspoon salt*
½ *teaspoon freshly ground black pepper*
3 *tablespoons red wine vinegar*
3 *tablespoons apricot jam or fruit chutney*
3 *large lemongrass leaves, bruised and chopped*

🦐 Using a pestle and mortar, crush the fennel, cumin, and cardamom seeds. Put them in a spice grinder, and grind to a fine powder. Mix with the turmeric, cayenne pepper, and garam masala.

🦐 Put the ginger root in a garlic press and squeeze the juice into the spices.

🦐 Heat the oil in a saucepan over a low heat. Add the spice mixture and gently fry for 3-5 minutes.

🦐 Add the onion and fry over medium heat for about 8 minutes, until golden. Stir in the garlic and fry for another minute or two.

🦐 Add the remaining marinade ingredients with 6 tablespoons of water. Simmer for a few minutes, until the mixture thickens slightly, then remove from the heat and leave until cold.

🦐 Put the lamb in a bowl and pour the marinade over it, stirring until evenly coated. Cover and leave in the refrigerator for at least four hours or overnight, stirring occasionally.

🦐 Remove the lamb from the marinade, reserving the marinade. Thread onto 8 skewers with the apricots, baby onions, and bay leaves. Lightly brush with oil.

🦐 Place on a rack over a barbecue or under a hot broilerl for 15-20 minutes, turning regularly, and brushing with oil.

🦐 Heat the reserved marinade in a small saucepan, and stir in the parsley. Serve with the kabobs.

Chicken Fajitas

• SERVES 4 •

Preparation time: 40 minutes, plus marinating

Cooking time: 15 minutes

12 ounces skinless chicken, cut into thin strips

peanut oil for frying

4 green onions (scallions), sliced

1 each sliced green, red, and yellow bell pepper

4 wheat flour tortillas, gently warmed

FOR THE MARINADE;

½ cup lite beer

1-2 fresh green chili peppers, seeded and chopped

1 garlic clove, crushed

2 tablespoons malt vinegar

¼ teaspoon ground cumin

salt and freshly ground black pepper

FOR THE SALSA:

2 tomatoes, seeded and finely chopped

2 tablespoons minced onion

1-3 fresh chili peppers, seeded and minced

2 tablespoons chopped fresh coriander (cilantro)

¼ teaspoon salt

1 teaspoon lime juice

Blend the marinade ingredients. Pour over the chicken and leave for at least 2 hours. Combine all the salsa ingredients, cover, and refrigerate.

Drain the chicken and reserve the marinade. Brown the chicken in 1 tablespoon of oil. Remove from the pan.

Fry the onions and bell peppers over medium until soft. Remove from the pan.

Add the marinade into the pan and simmer briskly until slightly reduced. Add the chicken and vegetables, stirring until heated through.

Spoon some chicken mixture and salsa down the middle of a warmed tortilla. Roll up and serve.

Beef Stir-Fry with Eggplant and Broccoli

• SERVES 4 •

Preparation time: 25 minutes, plus marinating

Cooking time: 15 minutes

12 ounces lean beef, cut into thin strips

3 tablespoons shoyu

10 Szechuan or black peppercorns, crushed

1 eggplant, cut into 1½-inch chunks

peanut oil for frying

4 thin slices fresh ginger root, minced

1 small dried red chili, seeded

2 garlic cloves, thinly sliced

2 red bell peppers, seeded and cut into squares

1 cup broccoli flowerets

⅓ cup light broth

1 tablespoon rice vinegar

½ teaspoon sugar

1 teaspoon sesame seeds

toasted sesame oil

Put the beef in a bowl and add 2 tablespoons of shoyu and the peppercorns. Set aside for 30 minutes.

Heat 2-3 tablespoons of oil in a wok, until almost smoking. Add the eggplant and stir-fry until just beginning to color. Remove from the pan and drain on paper towels.

Heat 2 teaspoons of oil and add the ginger, chili, and garlic. Stir once, then add the beef. Stir-fry over medium-high heat for 3 minutes. Remove the beef and juices.

Add the bell pepper and broccoli, and stir-fry for 4-5 minutes.

Return the beef and eggplant to the pan. Add the shoyu, broth, rice vinegar, and sugar. Stir-fry for 30 seconds over medium-high heat.

Sprinkle with sesame seeds and a dash of toasted sesame oil.

Venison Casserole with Red Wine, Orange, and Rosemary

This richly flavored casserole makes a healthy, low-fat dish for entertaining. According to Chinese medicine, serving red meat with green leafy vegetables helps make the protein easier to digest.

• SERVES 8 •

Preparation time: 25 minutes,
plus marinating and soaking
Cooking time: 3½ hours

2¼ pounds diced venison
1 cup navy beans, soaked overnight
3 tablespoons olive oil
2 onions, chopped
3 garlic cloves, chopped
4 carrots, thickly sliced
3 celery stalks, thickly sliced
7-ounce can chopped tomatoes
1½ cups home-made game or meat broth
2 tablespoons chopped fresh rosemary
1 teaspoon sea salt
freshly ground black pepper
4 tablespoons chopped flat-leafed parsley
finely grated zest of 1 orange
steamed leafy green vegetables and
crusty bread, to serve

FOR THE MARINADE:
2 tablespoons olive oil
3 garlic cloves, crushed
3-4 sprigs fresh rosemary
3-4 slivers orange peel without any white parts
1 small onion, sliced
3 tablespoons red wine vinegar
1¼ cups strong red wine
plenty of coarsely ground black pepper

🌿 Put the meat in a shallow dish. Combine all the marinade ingredients and pour over the meat. Cover and leave in the refrigerator overnight or for up to three days, turning occasionally. Remove from the marinade and pat dry with paper towels. Strain the marinade and reserve.

🌿 Drain the navy beans and put them in a saucepan with enough water to cover. Bring to the boil, then boil rapidly for 15 minutes. Simmer briskly for another 15 minutes, until just tender. Drain and set aside.

🌿 Heat the oil in a large flameproof casserole and brown the meat in batches. Remove with a perforated spoon.

🌿 Add the onions to the casserole, and gently fry over medium-low heat for 7-10 minutes, until softened. Add the garlic and fry until just golden.

🌿 Return the meat to the casserole with any juices. Stir in the cooked navy beans, carrots, celery, tomatoes, broth, rosemary, salt, and pepper. Strain the reserved marinade and add to the casserole. Bring to the boil, then cover, and simmer very gently for 2-2½ hours, until the meat is tender. Remove the lid during the last 15 minutes to allow the juices to reduce slightly.

🌿 Combine the parsley and orange zest, and stir into the casserole just before serving.

Vibrant Vegetables

VEGETABLE ACCOMPANIMENTS

With their freshness, color, and crisp, crunchy textures, vegetables are life itself, bringing nature's vitality to your plate. The link between good health and a diet based on plenty of vegetables is now firmly established, so we need to get in the habit of eating them as often as possible. Fortunately, one of the greatest delights of vegetable cookery is the enormous range of dishes that can be made with them.

As well as providing vital nutrients, vegetables add color and variety to the meal. A simple dish of potatoes, a crisp salad, or some plainly cooked green vegetables are usually all that's necessary to accompany a vegetarian meal. In meat-based meals, certain vegetables seem to have a natural affinity with a particular dish — red cabbage with pork or game, for instance. But on the whole, it's best to let your choice be guided by what looks fresh and lively in the store.

The art of preparing nutritious vegetables lies in the cooking. Plunged into a large pan of boiling water, green vegetables such as broccoli or green beans cook quickly with minimum loss of vitamins. Steaming is a gentler method best for roots and denser green vegetables, such as cauliflower or wedges of cabbage. Stir-frying over high heat is another way of retaining volatile vitamins.

Here we offer a selection of lively vegetable dishes guaranteed to retain their color, flavor, and nutrients. Cooked in large quantities and served with a grain dish, many of them will also make a delicious vegetarian entrée.

~ Tomatoes ~ and lycopene

Tomatoes and tomato products are the primary dietary source of lycopene, a carotenoid which gives them their red color. Recent studies strongly suggest that lycopene can protect against certain types of cancer — they can reduce the risk of prostate cancer by one-third. Lycopene may also be helpful to women. In animal tests, Japanese researchers have found that diets supplemented with lycopene significantly suppressed the development of breast cancer. Another study suggests that lyocpene may help to boost the immume system. Lycopene is found in significant amounts in pink-fleshed grapefruit, guavas, watermelon, and green onions (scallions), as well as in tomatoes, and is present in smaller amounts in dried apricots.

Stir-Fry of Yellow Peppers, Zucchini, and Tomatoes

Serve these vibrant, briefly cooked vegetables as a side dish with plain broiled meats or fish, or with a grain dish in a meat-free meal.

• SERVES 4 •

Preparation time: 20 minutes
Cooking time: 15 minutes
2 *tablespoons olive oil*
2 *small yellow bell peppers, cored, seeded, and cut into thin strips*
3-4 *baby purple onions, thinly sliced lengthwise*
12 *ounces mixed yellow and green zucchini, sliced*
2 *garlic cloves, minced*
1¾ *cups tomatoes, peeled, seeded, and diced*
2 *teaspoons cider vinegar*
salt and freshly ground black pepper
1 *tablespoon chopped flat-leafed parsley*

Heat the oil in a large skillet. Add the bell peppers, onions, and zucchini. Stir over medium-high heat, until just beginning to soften, then add the garlic. Reduce the heat a little, cover, and leave for 2-3 minutes.

Stir in the tomatoes, vinegar, salt, and black pepper. Cook, uncovered, for 3-4 minutes.

Tip the contents of the pan into a colander set over a bowl. Allow the juices to drain, then transfer the vegetables to a warmed serving dish.

Pour the juices back into the pan, bring to the boil, and simmer briskly, stirring, until reduced and slightly thickened. Pour this over the vegetables and sprinkle with parsley.

Broccoli, Carrots, and Sugar Snap Peas, with Lemon Zest and Olive Oil

A quickly made dish guaranteed to keep your broccoli looking bright green instead of an unappetizing yellow. The deeper the color of the vegetables, the higher the nutritional value. The broccoli stalks are too delicious to discard.

• SERVES 4 •

Preparation time: 10 minutes
Cooking time: 5 minutes
14 *ounces broccoli*
3 *carrots*
½ *cup sugar snap peas*
grated zest of 1 lemon
3 *tbsp snipped garlic chives*
sea salt flakes
olive oil

Discard the first 2 inches of the central broccoli stalk. Cut the remaining stems into thin diagonal slices. Break the flowerets into small pieces no bigger than 1½ inches in diameter. Thinly slice the carrots diagonally. Trim the sugar snap peas.

Put all the vegetables into a large saucepan of boiling salted water and bring back to the boil. Cook for 45 seconds, then drain immediately.

Put the vegetables back in the pan with the lemon zest and garlic chives. Sprinkle with sea salt flakes and drizzle with olive oil. Toss over medium heat until heated through.

~ Potatoes ~

The Chinese believe that the yin quality of potatoes improves one's receptive and compassionate nature, although eating too many of them can cause laziness. A baked potato in its jacket, or a plate of mashed potatoes, is certainly the most comforting of foods.

The fiber content of potatoes can help lubricate the intestines, and they are also a good source of vitamin B6. In oriental medicine, potatoes are valued for their neutral, soothing properties. They are rich in potassium and therefore a balancing food for people who use too much salt or eat salty foods. The juice from raw potatoes is a rich source of vitamin C, enzymes, and minerals. In 19th-century America, a poultice of raw grated potato was the remedy for drawing abscesses and carbuncles, and soothing eczema and swollen, sore eyes.

Sesame Roasted Roots

This earthy dish of root vegetables with butternut squash and baby onions is rich in slow-release carbohydrates, and this will leave you feeling contentedly replete for hours to come.

• SERVES 6 •

Preparation time: 15 minutes
Cooking time: 1 hour 10 minutes
1¾ pounds potatoes, peeled and cut into chunks
3 small rutabagas, peeled and halved lengthwise
5 ounces cerely root, peeled and cut into chunks
6 small Jerusalem artichokes, peeled
1 small butternut squash, peeled and cut into chunks
3 tablespoons light olive oil or peanut oil
2 tablespoons sesame seeds
1 tablespoon tamari (Japanese soy sauce)
6 small onions
salt and freshly ground black pepper
flat-leafed parsley, to garnish

🐾 Put the root vegetables and squash in a steamer basket with the rutabaga on top. Steam over boiling water for about 5 minutes, in batches if necessary, until just beginning to soften. Spread the vegetables out on a board or clean cloth and allow to dry.

🐾 Pour the oil into a roasting pan large enough to take the vegetables in a single layer, and heat until the oil is almost smoking in an oven preheated to 400°.

🐾 Add the sesame seeds and tamari, followed by all the vegetables including the onions, turning to coat evenly. Season, then roast for about 1 hour, until browned and crisp round the edges, turning frequently.

Garlic-Roasted Potatoes with Rosemary and Olives

An irresistible dish of crispy little cubes of potato with plenty of garlic, olives, and rosemary.

• SERVES 4 •

Preparation time: 20 minutes
Cooking time: 1 hour
2 pounds large potatoes
3 tablespoons light olive oil
pinch dried chili pepper flakes
1 tablespoon finely chopped fresh rosemary
3 tablespoons dry breadcrumbs
salt and freshly ground black pepper
4-6 large cloves unpeeled garlic, slightly crushed
6 black olives, pitted and sliced
chopped flat-leafed parsley, to garnish

🐾 Cook the potatoes in their skins in boiling water for 10-12 minutes, until only just tender. Drain well, then remove the skins when cool enough to handle. Cut into 1-inch cubes and put in a roasting pan.

🐾 Combine the oil, chili pepper flakes, rosemary, breadcrumbs, salt, and pepper. Pour the mixture over the potatoes, turning them to coat.

🐾 Roast in a preheated oven at 425° for about 30-35 minutes, turning occasionally, until evenly browned and crisp. Add the garlic and roast for another 10-15 minutes.

🐾 Peel the garlic and transfer with the potatoes to a warmed serving dish. Scatter the olives and parsley over the dish before serving.

~ Carrots ~ pumpkins, and alpha-carotene

Until relatively recently, beta-carotene was thought to be the substance in orange-fleshed vegetables that reduced the risk of cancer. However, the most recent research suggests that alpha-carotene is the more dominant protective factor for some cancers. Two American studies suggest that it could significantly reduce the risk of lung cancer, and earlier Japanese tests on animals have shown that it could inhibit the growth of cancer cells in the liver, lungs, and skin. Alpha-carotene is present in large amounts in carrots and pumpkin, regardless of whether raw, frozen, or cooked. It is thought that just one carrot a day is a cancer-protective dose. In oriental medicine, carrots have always been valued for their beneficial action on the lungs, for easing whooping cough, and coughs in general, and for their ability to dissolve stones and tumors.

Algerian Carrots

This is a great way of livening up a dish of carrots. Lemon juice cuts their sweetness and mint gives the dish a lovely refreshing flavor. This vegetable dish is good with poultry or white fish, and very rich in carotenes.

• SERVES 4 •

Preparation time: 10 minutes
Cooking time: 15 minutes
1¼ pounds carrots, sliced diagonally
½-1 teaspoon harissa (hot sauce)
2 tablespoons light olive oil
3 garlic cloves, thinly sliced
juice of 1 lemon
2 teaspoons cumin seeds, toasted and crushed
½ teaspoon salt
½ teaspoon sugar
2 tablespoons chopped fresh mint

🍃 Put the carrots in a steamer basket set over boiling water. Steam for about 5 minutes, until barely tender. Reserve the cooking water and mix 5 tablespoons of it with the harissa (hot sauce).
🍃 Heat the oil in a skillet over medium heat. Add the garlic, harissa, lemon juice, cumin, salt, and sugar, and mix well. Add the carrots, then cover and cook over a medium-low heat for about 10 minutes, until the liquid is reduced.
🍃 Stir in the mint and serve at once.

Green Bean, Pumpkin, and Okra Stir-Fry

• SERVES 4-6 •

Preparation time: 15 minutes
Cooking time: 15 minutes
⅔ cup okra
6 ounces stringless green beans
4 tablespoons peanut oil
¼-½ teaspoon dried chili pepper flakes
½ teaspoon mustard seeds
½ teaspoon cumin seeds
1 teaspoon salt
1-2 teaspoons ground turmeric
½ teaspoon sugar
½ teaspoon garam masala or curry powder
7 ounces pumpkin or butternut squash, peeled and cut into chunks
7-ounce can chopped tomatoes
1 tablespoon chopped fresh coriander (cilantro)

🍃 Trim the stems from the okra, taking care not to cut into the seed chambers. Cut the beans into 1½-inch pieces.
🍃 Plunge the okra and beans into boiling water. Bring back to the boil and cook for 30 seconds. Drain and set aside.
🍃 Heat the oil in a large skillet. Add the chili pepper flakes and mustard and cumin seeds. When the mustard seeds begin to pop, add the salt, turmeric, sugar, and garam masala. Stir-fry for 30 seconds.
🍃 Add the pumpkin and stir-fry over medium heat until beginning to brown. Stir in the okra and beans. Cover and cook over low heat for 3-5 minutes, until just tender, stirring occasionally.
🍃 Stir in the tomatoes and cook, uncovered, for 5 minutes more. Sprinkle with coriander (cilantro).

Sweet Offerings

DESSERTS

Desserts satisfy a deep-seated desire for something sweet, and they make us feel good. As long as they are not loaded with fats and sugar, a well-made dessert can have therapeutic properties. They are a useful way of rounding off a protein-rich meal with food of a lighter quality; and they can add substance to a light meal — for instance, a midweek lunch could consist of a salad and a dessert.

Why not eat a dessert on its own as a mid-afternoon snack, or later on in the evening if dinner has been particularly early, or even for breakfast? Treating a dessert as a little meal in its own right is one of the best ways of serving them.

Desserts containing spices and herbs, as they did in days gone by, can act as a digestive aid. Mint, bay, cardamom, saffron, and ginger are all useful in this respect. Desserts based on low-fat dairy products, such as ricotta cheese or yogurt, are a valuable source of calcium, especially after a meal that may have been lacking in this important mineral.

Healthiest and most mouthwatering of all are desserts based on fruits. Packed with vitamins, minerals, and fiber, fruits are the perfect ingredients for desserts that are every bit as tempting as those based on excessive and unhealthy amounts of cream and sugar.

The desserts that follow include stunning fruit salads flavored with unusual herbs and spices, simple fruit purées, and a decadent chocolate torte. All of them will delight the eye and the palate without putting on the pounds.

~ Herbs ~ and spices

Herbs and spices count among nature's most potent healers, standing somewhere between a medicine and a food. The texts of Ayurveda, India's ancient system of medicine, refer to the "yoga of herbs," meaning the "right usage" of flavors in what we eat to promote well-being and good health. Combined with appropriate herbs and spices, vegetables, grains, pulses, and even fruits take on a new vibrancy. For example, street vendors in India sell slices of fruit flavored with all kinds of spices, including salt and pepper. The spices used will often be those known to stimulate digestion — ginger, mint, or fennel, for instance. The Mexicans sell a fiery combination of juicy orange halves sprinkled with chopped chili peppers. This is a surprisingly refreshing snack in a hot climate — chili peppers not only aid digestion but induce sweating, to cool the body.

Salad of Vine Fruits with Ginger, Chili, and Mint Syrup

Vine fruits include not only grapes but melons, kiwifruits, and passion fruits too, which combine to make a luscious fruit salad. This is good to serve after a heavy meal since ginger, chili, and mint all help the digestive process.

• SERVES 6 •

Preparation time: 20 minutes, plus cooling

Cooking time: 10 minutes

1 small orange-fleshed melon such as
Charentais or Cantaloupe

3 kiwifruits

1¼ cups black grapes

sprigs of mint, to decorate

FOR THE SYRUP:

½ cup sugar

1¼ cups water

2 thinly pared strips lime peel

3 thin slices fresh ginger root

1 fresh green chili pepper, seeded

4 sprigs of mint

🦐 To make the syrup, put the sugar and water in a small saucepan with the remaining ingredients. Stir over low heat until the sugar has dissolved, then boil for 5-7 minutes, until syrupy. Leave to cool, then strain.

🦐 Scoop the melon into balls with a melon-baller. Put in a serving bowl with any juice.

🦐 Peel the kiwifruits and thinly slice crosswise, then cut in half. Add to the melon.

🦐 Halve the grapes, remove the seeds if necessary, and add to the rest of the fruits.

🦐 Pour the syrup over the fruits, cover, and chill. Decorate with mint sprigs before serving.

Compôte of Dark Fruits with Bay Syrup

A dramatically colored fruit compôte, enigmatically flavored with bay leaves. If pomegranates are out of season, use another small jewel-like fruit such as wild strawberries or other red berries, such as ollalieberries. Serve at room temperature to appreciate the flavor.

• SERVES 6 - 8 •

Preparation time: 25 minutes

Cooking time: 10 minutes

1¼ pounds black-skinned plums such as
Angelino or Santa Rosa

1¼ cups black cherries, pitted

1 cup seedless black grapes

½ cup pomegranate seeds (arils)

1 tablespoon almonds with skin, halved lengthwise

fresh bay leaf, to decorate

FOR THE SYRUP:

1 cup sugar sugar

2½ cups water

2-3 thinly pared strips orange peel

8 fresh bay leaves

🦐 Cut the plums all the way round the indentation through to the stone. Twist the halves in opposite directions, then scoop out the stone. Cut the halves into quarters, then into thin segments. Put them in a heatproof serving bowl.

🦐 Put the syrup ingredients in a small saucepan. Stir over gentle heat until the sugar has dissolved, then boil for 7-10 minutes, until slightly syrupy. Immediately strain the boiling syrup over the plums. Leave to cool but do not chill.

🦐 Add the cherries, grapes, and pomegranate seeds to the plums, and sprinkle with the almonds.

Since the days of the Maya and Aztecs, and its "discovery" by the Spanish conquistadores, chocolate has always been highly valued as a sustaining food. We now know that it is the carbohydrates and fats in chocolate that provide fuel for the body. Claims that chocolate is bad for you are almost certainly to do with the vegetable fats and excess sugar added to mediocre, mass-produced chocolate. Good-quality dark chocolate contains little or no sugar, plenty of valuable minerals, and B vitamins. Chocolate also contains chemicals tcalled endorphins, which are thought to affect the brain — possibly causing a lift in mood and a creation of positive energy. As long as you don't binge, chocolate deserves a place on the list of therapeutic foods, not only for its ability to revive flagging energy but also for the pleasure it brings.

Papaya and Pistachio Chocolate Torte with Ginger Ricotta Cream

This seemingly decadent torte is a dessert for a special occasion — and yet it's very low in fat.

• SERVES 8-10 •

Preparation time: 45 minutes, plus chilling
Cooking time: 10 minutes
6 tablespoons flour
1 teaspoon double-acting baking powder
3 tablespoons unsweetened cocoa powder
⅛ teaspoon salt
2 tablespoons ground almonds
3 large eggs, plus 2 egg whites
½ cup superfine sugar
1 ripe papaya (about 1 pound)
1 tablespoon shelled pistachio nuts
sifted confectioner's sugar, for dusting

FOR THE GINGER RICOTTA CREAM:

¾ cup low-fat ricotta cheese
1 tablespoon low-fat plain yogurt
1 teaspoon sugar, or to taste
1-inch piece fresh ginger root, peeled

🐦 Grease and line a 13 x 9-inch jellyroll pan with nonstick baking parchment.

🐦 Sift flour, baking powder, cocoa powder, and salt into a bowl. Add the ground almonds and stir.

🐦 In a large bowl, whisk the whole eggs with the sugar for 5 minutes. The mixture should leave a definite trail when the whisk is lifted. Fold in the flour mixture.

🐦 In another bowl, whisk the egg whites until stiff but not dry.

🐦 Using a metal spoon, carefully fold one-third of the egg white into the flour mixture, then fold in the rest.

🐦 Spoon into the pan, leveling the surface. Bake in a preheated oven at 400° for 10-12 minutes, until springy to touch. Leave in the pan for a few minutes, then invert the cake onto a wire rack. Peel off the baking parchment and leave to cool.

🐦 To make the ricotta cream, put the ricotta, yogurt, and sugar in a blender. Put the ginger in a garlic press and squeeze the juice into the blender. Blend until very smooth.

🐦 Halve the papaya and scoop out the seeds. Cut into quarters lengthwise and peel. Roughly chop one quarter and mash to a slightly chunky purée. Stir this into the ricotta cream. Refrigerate for 30 minutes or more.

🐦 Set aside one of the remaining papaya quarters and chop the rest into small cubes.

🐦 Cover the pistachio nuts with boiling water and leave for 5 minutes. Slip off the skins and chop the nuts.

🐦 Cut the cake crosswise into three rectangles. Lay them on top of each other and trim the edges neatly.

🐦 Spread half the cream mixture over one rectangle. Scatter with half the chopped papaya and one-third of the pistachio nuts. Place the second rectangle on top. Spread with the remaining cream and scatter with the remaining chopped papaya and a sprinkling of pistachios. Put the last rectangle of cake on top, press gently, and dust with confectioner's sugar.

🐦 Cut the remaining piece of papaya crosswise into thin slices and arrange on top. Scatter with the remaining pistachios.

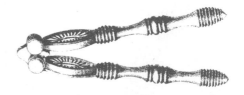

~ Pomegranates ~

The leathery yellow or red skin conceals tightly packed clumps of crimson, jewel-like seeds, known as arils, bursting with juice. Pomegranates are worth buying for their natural beauty alone. In many parts of the world, they are a traditional symbol of fertility. Pomegranates contain plenty of potassium, as well as glucose and fructose — natural sugars which help stabilize blood sugar levels. They are also a rich source of vitamin C. In Chinese medicine, pomegranates are believed to fortify what is known as weak or empty blood (anemia), and to cheer the spirit. The Chinese also believe that they destroy intestinal worms, strengthen the gums, and soothe mouth ulcers. In the Indian system of Ayurvedic medicine, pomegranates are used to cure dysentery, vomiting, dyspepsia, to cleanse the mouth and throat, and to purify the blood.

Rice Pudding with Dried Fruits and Pomegranates

A deceptively rich and sweet dessert based on an Indian recipe — to be eaten in small quantities.

• SERVES 6 •

Preparation time: 25 minutes
Cooking time: 1 hour 5 minutes
2 tablespoons long-grain white rice,
soaked in cold water for 30 minutes
2 tablespoons clarified butter
1 fresh bay leaf
2 quarts low-fat or 2% milk
2 tablespoons sugar
seeds from 3 cardamom pods
2 cloves
2-inch cinnamon stick
2 tablespoons seedless raisins
¼ cup finely chopped dried Hunza or
ordinary apricots
seeds from 1 pomegranate
2 tablespoons flaked almonds, toasted

🍃 Drain the rice and pat dry with paper towels.

🍃 Heat the butter in a large sauté pan. Add the rice, and stir for a minute or so, until the rice darkens slightly. Do not let the rice burn.

🍃 Add the bay leaf and milk, and bring to the boil, stirring. Reduce the heat slightly and leave to boil for 30 minutes, stirring now and again, or until reduced by about half.

🍃 Stir in the sugar, cardamom, cloves, cinnamon, raisins, and apricots. Simmer over medium-low heat, stirring occasionally, for 25-30 minutes, until very thick and creamy and reduced to about one-third of its original volume.

🍃 Pour into individual dishes. Sprinkle with pomegranate seeds and almonds.

🍃 Serve warm, at room temperature, or chilled.

Mango and Blood Orange Whip

A super-healthy dessert bursting with beta-carotene and vitamin C. If blood oranges are out of season, use two small ordinary oranges instead.

• SERVES 4 •

Preparation time: 25 minutes, plus chilling
2 blood oranges
3 mangoes, about 1¾ pounds total weight
2 tablespoons sugar
1-inch piece fresh ginger root, minced
2 tablespoons lime juice
⅔ cup low-fat thickset yogurt
toasted coconut ribbons and shredded lime zest,
to decorate

🍃 Using a small sharp knife, remove the rind and all the white parts from the oranges. Working over a sieve placed over a bowl, remove the flesh by slicing between each segment and the membrane. Reserve the flesh and juice.

🍃 With the narrow side facing you, slice vertically down one side of each mango about 1 inch away from the center, just missing the stone. Repeat with the other side. Cut off any bits of flesh still attached to the stone.

🍃 Remove the skin and chop the mango flesh. Put in a blender with the orange flesh and reserved juices, sugar, ginger, and lime juice. Blend until smooth, adding more lime juice if necessary.

🍃 Pour into individual serving bowls. Swirl in the yogurt. Cover and chill until ready to serve.

🍃 Decorate with toasted coconut ribbons and shreds of lime zest.

Pear and Berry Purée with Rosemary Shortbread

This is a slightly time-consuming dessert but worth making for a special occasion. You could make the pear purée on its own for an everyday meal. The shortbread contains half the fat normally used but is still crisp and crunchy — a delicious contrast to the purée. Rosemary adds a mysterious touch to the flavor, but can be omitted if you prefer.

• SERVES 4 •

Preparation time: 45 minutes, plus chilling
Cooking time: 40 minutes
4-5 *juicy pears*
3 *tablespoons sugar*
⅔ *cup dry white wine*
1 *vanilla bean, split*
seeds from 6 cardamom pods, lightly crushed
3 *tablespoons lemon juice*
1½ *cups dark berry fruits such as black raspberries,*
blueberries, and blackberries, stems removed
2 *tablespoons confectioner's sugar*
fresh berries, to decorate

FOR THE ROSEMARY
SHORTBREAD:
1 *tablespoon minced fresh rosemary*
2 *tablespoons sugar*
1 *cup all-purpose flour*
¼ *cup rice flour*
pinch of salt
¼ *cup butter*
1 *egg yolk*
1 *tablespoon milk*

🌿 Quarter, core, and peel the pears. Put them in a saucepan with the sugar, wine, vanilla bean, cardamom, and lemon juice. Bring to the boil, then cover and simmer for 7-10 minutes, or until slightly translucent.

🌿 Lift out the pears with a perforated spoon and put them in a blender. Heat the juices in the pan until they boil, to reduce them slightly. Strain 2-3 tablespoons of syrup over the pears, and purée until smooth. Allow to cool, then chill.

🌿 Put the berries and confectioner's sugar in a blender, and blend until smooth. Press through a fine-meshed sieve into a jug. Cover and chill.

🌿 To make the shortbread, pound the rosemary and sugar in a mortar with a pestle. Sift the flours and salt into a bowl, then rub in the butter. Mix the egg yolk and milk, and stir into the mixture with the sugar and rosemary. Knead into a lump. Turn out on to a board sprinkled with rice flour and form into a smooth circle 8 inches in diameter. Press into a mold or pinch the edges with your fingers. Place on a greased cookie sheet and prick all over with a fork. Bake in a preheated oven at 350° for 20-25 minutes, until firm to touch. Mark into thin segments and allow to cool on the cookie sheet.

🌿 Pour the pear purée into four sundae glasses and pour the berry purée over the top. Decorate with a few fresh berries and serve with the rosemary shortbread.

Sunset Soothers

I f your evening meal has been reasonably early, the chances are that by bedtime you might be feeling in need of a little sustenance. After all, there is nothing more dispiriting than trying to settle down to sleep feeling hungry. By late evening, you need to feel comfortably replete, but not so full that the body is still digesting in the early hours.

What's needed at this hour are the sweetish, easily digested snacks and desserts loved by children. A simple gelatin dessert, some dried fruit, or yogurt sweetened with fruit purée or honey are all ideal.

If you've had a busy day and are having trouble winding down, taking a little time to prepare yourself a glass of delicious fresh fruit or vegetable juice can be very therapeutic. Fruits such as pineapple and papaya contain digestive enzymes that help break down proteins, and juices made with these may be helpful after an evening meal based on meat or fish.

Vegetable juices made with lettuce or celery can have a mild sedative effect, and these are helpful if you are under stress. Herb teas are cleansing and digestive, and some of them are also conducive to sleep — chamomile is well known, but dried orange blossom or lime flowers are equally effective.

The recipes that follow include ideas for juices, hot drinks, simple candy, and desserts. They are all designed to help you end your day feeling relaxed, ready for sleep, and comfortably nourished.

~ Raw juices ~

Raw juices can play a vital role in promoting and maintaining health and vitality. Drinking them on a regular basis is a convenient way of getting a potent cocktail of nutrients into the system. However, the process of juicing removes much of the beneficial fiber content of fruits and vegetables. Juices are bursting with quickly absorbed enzymes, vitamins, and minerals. If there is a particular vitamin or mineral that you want to increase, then choose the appropriate fruit or vegetable (see pages 116-123.) Make sure your fruits and vegetables are of top quality and absolutely fresh. Organic produce is best, as it contains no harmful pesticide residues. Use a centrifugal juicer for the best results — it squeezes out all the juice from the fiber. A food processor will do a reasonable job but it cannot extract juice from the pulp.

Papaya and Pineapple Juice

Packed with vitamin C, this is an excellent drink after a late evening meal. Papaya is a traditional remedy for indigestion because of its naturally occurring enzymes.

• SERVES 1 •

Preparation time: 10 minutes
½ *papaya, peeled, seeds removed*
9-*ounce chunk peeled pineapple*
1-2 *teaspoons lime juice*

If using a centrifugal juicer, follow the manufacturer's instructions. Otherwise, roughly chop the prepared fruits and put them in a food processor. Add the lime juice, then grind the flesh to a pulp. Press out the juice through a fine sieve. Thin the juice with water if preferred.

Apple and Grape Juice

This vitamin C-rich juice oxidizes very quickly, so drink it immediately after juicing.

• SERVES 1 •

Preparation time: 10 minutes
2 *green-skinned apples*
3 *tablespoons lemon juice*
3 *ounces seedless green grapes*

If using a centrifugal juicer, follow the manufacturer's instructions. Otherwise, quarter and core the apples but do not peel them. Cut into thin slices and sprinkle with some of the lemon juice. Put in a food processor with the grapes and the rest of the lemon juice. Grind to a pulp, then press out the juice through a fine sieve.

Celery and Lettuce Juice

Oriental healers have used celery to treat high blood pressure, while lettuce has been used for centuries as a sedative. Lettuce was also recommended by Culpeper, the 17th-century herbalist, to "abate bodily lust."

• SERVES 1 •

Preparation time: 10 minutes
8 *ounces tender celery stalks, leaves included*
8 *ounces lettuce leaves, both inner and outer,*
thick stalks removed

If using a centrifugal juicer, follow the manufacturer's instructions. Otherwise, cut the celery into chunks, tear the lettuce into small pieces, and put in a food processor. Grind to a pulp. Press out the juice through a fine sieve.

Foods for Health and Healing

THE NUTRIENTS IN FOODS

The nutrients in foods have a specific task to perform within the body. Without them, we are likely to suffer from some kind of abnormality or deficiency disease, but with an abundant supply of particular nutrients, we may actually alleviate or even prevent certain diseases.

How much do I need?

Unless you are an expert, it is often hard to know for sure whether you are getting the right amount of a particular nutrient. In order to provide a yardstick — and it is no more than that — government nutritional experts use various terms by which to refer to the quantity of food nutrients that should be eaten every day to ensure good health. In the US, one of the several terms used is the Recommended Daily Allowance (RDA).

However, it is not as simple as that. Everyone has different nutritional requirements, and the amounts needed may change depending on what is going on in your life. If you are under a lot of stress, or there is some aspect of your health you want to work on nutritionally, then your needs are going to differ from the norm.

In order to improve and protect your health, you certainly need to be aware of the recommended daily intake, and, even more important, to have some sense of how your nutrient intake is shaping up relative to this. Excess amounts of certain nutrients can be injurious to health. For example, too much vitamin A can cause vomiting, abnormal bone growth, bone and joint pain, liver damage, and potential birth defects. Vitamin D is especially toxic to young children, and excess amounts can lead to kidney stones, excess bleeding, weak bones, and calcium deposits in soft tissue, which in turn can cause renal and cardiovascular damage.

Where the eldery are mentioned under the "special needs" categories in the following entries in this section, this does not denote that they require more nutrients, but that they are less likely to obtain the required amounts in their normal daily diet. In general, the RDAs given for each nutrient are per day for the 19-50 age group.

CARBOHYDRATES

RDA *50% of total calories* NSP 18*g*

There are three major groups of carbohydrates: sugars, starches, and nonstarch polysaccharides (NSP).

Sugars include glucose and fructose, found in fruit and vegetables; sucrose, found in sugar cane and beets, and some fruits and root vegetables; and lactose, found in milk.

Starches, found in flour and potatoes, are indigestible when eaten raw.

NSP, collectively known as dietary fiber, are found in the cell walls of plant foods. The NSP in wheat, corn, and rice consist of cellulose and related substances. NSP in fruits, vegetables, oats, barley, and rye contain pectins and gums as well.

Function: Carbohydrates provide the fuel to produce the energy needed for normal body functions, physical exercise, and work. Starchy foods provide slow-release energy and stabilize blood sugar levels. Cellulose NSP binds with the feces, easing their passage through the intestines and helping to prevent constipation. Pectin-based NSP can help reduce blood cholesterol.

Deficiency: Since staple foods are starch-based, deficiencies are unlikely. Low intakes of NSP are associated with increased risk of bowel disorders.

Risks: Certain types of sugary foods are associated with tooth decay. Because of their bulky nature, there is a small risk that, if eaten to excess, NSP-rich foods may prevent small children eating enough to satisfy energy needs.

Special needs: People on low-fat diets, people who are obese, people who exercise intensively and perform hard physical work. Main sources: Grains, pulses, bread, pasta, root vegetables, squash, plantains, fruits.

FATS

RDA *No more than 30% of total calories, of which no more than 10% to come from saturates*

Fats and oils consist mainly of compounds called triglycerides, which comprise three fatty acids and a unit of glycerol. There are three types of fatty acids — polyunsaturated, monounsaturated, and saturated.

All fats contain both saturated and unsaturated fatty acids, but if the proportion of saturates is greater, then the fat is said to be saturated, and vice versa. Some foods can have roughly equal amounts. As a general rule, saturated fats are solid at room temperature and tend to come from animal sources, while unsaturated fats are usually liquid at room temperature and come from plant foods (except some tropical oils).

Function: Polyunsaturated fats in fish oils and vegetable oils are a rich, natural source of the fat-soluble vitamins A, D, E, and K, and are also necessary for their absorption. Poly- and monounsaturates can help lower blood cholesterol levels. The polyunsaturates found in oily fish (omega-3 fatty acids) reduce the tendency of the blood to clot.

Deficiency: Unlikely.

Risks: A high-fat diet increases the risk of heart disease, obesity, cancer, and a host of other "modern" ailments. Saturated fats can cause the blood to thicken and clot more easily, and raise blood cholesterol levels, increasing the risk of a heart attack or stroke. Increased blood cholesterol is far more crucial in relation to heart disease than cholesterol from foods.

Special needs: Children aged two years and under need a higher fat diet than others.

Main sources of saturated fat: Beef, lamb, pork, poultry, dairy products, eggs, coconut oil, palm oil.

Main sources of monounsaturated fat: Beef, lamb, pork, poultry, white fish, oily fish, seafood, eggs, avocados, olives, nuts and nut oils, palm oil.

Main sources of polyunsaturated fat: White fish, oily fish, soya milk, nuts, margarine, nuts and nut oils, vegetable oils, seed oils.

Stability: Some oils and fats oxidize at very high temperatures. They can also become rancid.

PROTEIN

RDA *Women: 46-50g Men: 58-63g*

Proteins are complex molecules made up of chains of amino-acids. A typical protein may contain 500 or more amino-acids, eight of which are essential since the body cannot make them for itself. The arrangement of amino-acids within the molecule determines the function and characteristics of the protein. Protein from plant foods usually has a lower nutritional value because one or more of the essential amino-acids are missing. However, when plant foods from different sources are combined — pulses with grains, for instance — the amino-acid pattern is improved. Because of this, it is important for vegetarians to eat a wide variety of foods.

Function: Protein is an essential nutrient needed mainly for the growth of body tissues in babies and children, and for the repair and replacement of tissues in adults. It is used as a source of energy when carbohydrates and fat stores in the body are very low.

Deficiency: Unlikely in the West, but babies and young children in underdeveloped countries suffer from a range of disorders known as protein energy malnutrition.

Risks: Very high doses may aggravate poor kidney function.

Special needs: Babies, young children, pregnant, and lactating women, people recovering from injury or surgical operations. Vegetarian and vegan diets tend to be low in protein, due to a lack of animal products.

Main sources: Dairy products, eggs, meat, fish, poultry, legumes (particularly soybeans and soybean products such as tofu), grains and grain products, nuts, seeds, dried sea vegetables.

Stability: Methionine, an amino-acid found in milk, eggs, and beef, may be reduced during cooking. Collagen, a meat protein, dissolves in the liquids that drip from meat as it cooks.

VITAMIN A

RDA *Women. 800µg Men: 1000µg*

Also known as retinol, vitamin A is found in foods from animal sources, but can also be made from carotenes found in plant foods, which convert to vitamin A in the body. It is fat-soluble and stored in the liver.

Function: Vitamin A plays an important part in the efficiency of many body functions. It is essential for normal color vision and for the cells within the eye which enable us to see in dim light. As well as being vital for children's growth, vitamin A helps protect the skin and mucous membranes, such as those lining the mouth, nose, breathing passages, and the gut. Vitamin A from carotenes is an important antioxidant which may help reduce the risk of some cancers.

Deficiency: Deficiency is rare in developed countries since the amount in the liver of a well-nourished adult can supply the body's needs for several months. That said, poor night vision is one of the first signs. Dry skin can be another sign. Serious deficiency leads to drying and damage of the eye, which may eventually cause blindness.

Risks: Carotenes are non-toxic, but excessive doses of retinol taken over long periods can lead to liver and bone damage. If you are pregnant, you should not take vitamin A supplements.

Special needs: Lactating women need slightly more.

Main sources of retinol: Liver, milk, oily fish, fish oils, egg yolk, butter, margarine.

Main sources of carotene: Orange-fleshed fruits and vegetables, bell peppers, and dark-green leafy vegetables.

Stability: Both retinol and carotene are stable throughout most cooking processes, although there is some loss when frying butter or margarine at high temperatures. Losses also occur in the presence of oxygen and light, so keep your carrots in the dark.

B VITAMINS

The B vitamins are a group of almost a dozen different substances. They each have their own role within the body, but they work as a team. They are all water-soluble.

Thiamin (B1)

RDA Women: 1.1mg Men: 1.5mg

Function: Needed for the release of energy from carbohydrates, and for healthy nerve and muscle function.

Deficiency: Rare, but can be found in chronic alchoholics. Severe deficiency causes beri-beri, which affects nerves and muscle function.

Risks: The body excretes excess amounts, therefore it is unlikely to cause undesirable side-effects.

Special needs: Pregnant and lactating women, individuals on high-carbohydrate diets, heavy drinkers.

Main sources: Bread, flour, yeast, most breakfast cereals, meat (especially pork), potatoes, pulses, liver, brewer's yeast, enriched grains.

Stability: Thiamin is one of the least stable vitamins, losing up to 50% during cooking at high temperatures. It is also destroyed by baking soda.

Riboflavin (B2)

RDA Women: 1.3mg Men:1.7mg

Function: Needed for the release of energy from proteins, fats, and carbohydrates, and for growth.

Deficiency: Signs are dry, flaky skin, splits at the corners of the mouth, skin changes, and eye disorders.

Risks: Excess amounts are not known to be toxic, since it is poorly absorbed.

Special needs: Pregnant and lactating women, and anyone with increased energy expenditure and energy requirements.

Main sources: Meat (particularly beef and liver), kidney, milk, eggs, fish, yeast, cheese, enriched grains, green vegetables.

Stability: Leaches into cooking water and meat juices. Unstable when cooked with baking soda, and especially sensitive to light. Choose milk packaged in opaque containers, which minimizes light sensitivity and leaching of nutrients.

Niacin (B3)

RDA Women: 15mg Men: 19mg

Two related substances — nicotinic acid and nicotinamide — are both called niacin.

Function: Needed for energy release in cells. Helps maintain healthy nervous and digestive systems.

Deficiency: Rare in the US but still widespread in some underdeveloped countries. Leads to pellagra which causes skin rashes, diarrhea, and dementia.

Risks: Excessively high doses may cause flushed skin, rashes, and liver damage.

Special needs: During the last months of pregnancy and when lactating.

Main sources: Meat, poultry, fish, liver, kidney, yeast, milk, cheese, eggs, nuts, peanut butter.

Stability: Niacin is stable under heat, but losses occur when food is blanched.

Pantothenic acid (B5)

RDA None specified. Normal daily intake 5-20mg

Function: Needed for the release of energy from carbohydrates, protein, and fats. Contributes to cell growth, the production of steroid hormones, and essential fatty acids.

Deficiency: Unlikely.

Risks: An excess can lead to diarrhea and water retention.

Special needs: Following injury and surgical operations.

Main sources: Meat, poultry, fish, liver, yeast, egg white, grains, pulses, whole grains, vegetables.

Stability: Reasonably stable during cooking and storage. Can be lost in thawing and cooking frozen meat.

Pyridoxine (B6)

RDA *Women: 1.6mg Men: 2.0mg*

Function: Needed for protein metabolism, and maintaining a healthy nervous system, skin, muscles, and blood. Boosts the immune system. Some studies suggest that it decreases the symptoms of pre-menstrual conditions.

Deficiency: Rare, but can lead to skin problems, irritability, muscle weakness, as well as depression and mental convulsions in infants.

Risks: Impaired function of sensory nerves. Long-term very high doses can be toxic.

Special needs: Pregnant and lactating women, women taking a contraceptive pill, heavy drinkers, elderly people.

Main sources: Meat (particularly pork), poultry, fish, liver, kidneys, yeast, egg white, milk, grains, pulses, nuts, green vegetables.

Stability: Sensitive to high temperatures in cooking, light, and long -term freezing.

Folic acid

RDA *Women: 180μg Men: 200μg*

Function: Vital for the formation of new cells and therefore for growth of the fetus and normal development in children. Works with vitamin B12 to make hemoglobin in red blood cells, and boosts immunity function. Helps reduce the risk of neural tube defects. New evidence suggests that folic acid can prevent death from heart disease. Folates are compounds derived from folic acid.

Deficiency: Can lead to megaloblastic anemia in young children and pregnant women, and impaired growth.

Risks: Unlikely, but may lead to reduced zinc absorption. Large doses can mask a vitamin B12 deficiency.

Special needs: Pregnant and lactating women, babies and young children, heavy drinkers, women taking the contraceptive pill, elderly people.

Main sources: Leafy green vegetables, whole-wheat bread, liver, oranges.

Stability: Easily destroyed during long storage. Up to 50% can be lost during cooking.

Cyanocobalamin (B12)

RDA *Women and Men: 2.0μg*

Function: Needed for production of red blood cells, healthy nerves, and growth.

Deficiency: Vegans are at particular risk, since the vitamin is mainly found in animal foods. Deficiency is otherwise unlikely since adequate supplies are stored in the liver, but may result in anemia, nerve damage, or a smooth tongue.

Risks: Unlikely.

Special needs: Elderly people, pregnant, and lactating women, vegans, people suffering from anaemia.

Main sources: Liver, meat, poultry, fish, eggs, milk, cheese, yeast.

Stability: Losses can occur during cooking and storage.

VITAMIN C

RDA *Women and Men: 60mg*

Unlike most animals, humans cannot make vitamin C for themselves and therefore need a regular supply. Animal tissues are saturated with the vitamin and there has been considerable, and as yet unresolved, debate as to whether our intake should be high enough to reach the same state of saturation.

Function: Helps the white blood cells fight infection, and assists with the absorption of iron from food. It speeds up wound healing, helps produce collagen and keeps gums healthy. Vitamin C is an important antioxidant, protecting the body from the harmful effect of free radicals, and thus helps to reduce the risk of cancer.

Deficiency: Can leave you more susceptible to infection, slow down wound healing and cause bleeding gums. A severe deficiency results in scurvy.

Risks: High intakes sometimes result in diarrhea and kidney stones.

Special needs: Elderly people, people who do not eat fruit and vegetables, people who eat a lot of processed foods, heavy drinkers, smokers, pregnant, and lactating women.

Main sources: Fresh fruits (particularly tropical fruits), vegetables (particularly bell and chili peppers and dark-green leafy vegetables).

Stability: Lost during cooking, long-term deep freezing, and exposure to light.

VITAMIN D

RDA *Women and Men 5-10μg*

Vitamin D is produced in the body by the action of sunlight on the skin, and it is also supplied in food. If you live in a part of the country where winter makes itself felt, you can build up enough vitamin D in the liver during the spring, summer, and fall to last you the rest of the year, provided your skin is regularly exposed to the sun from April through October.

Function: Needed for calcium absorption and for strong, healthy bones and teeth, as well as for phosphorus absorption. Individuals with osteoarthritis may benefit from a larger intake of vitamin D.

Deficiency: Can lead to defective bone growth in children, and osteomalacia and osteoporosis in adults.

Risks: Since vitamin D is stored in the liver, high doses are dangerous especially for babies and young children. Overdosage can result in weak bones, excess bleeding, and kidney stones.

Special needs: Children under five and lactating women, housebound people, people who are not exposed to sunlight because of cultural dress restrictions, elderly people.

Main dietary sources: Oily fish, fish oils, butter, margarine, cheese, evaporated milk, eggs.

Stability: Vitamin D is stable during normal cooking.

VITAMIN E

RDA *Women: 8mg Men: 10mg*

Many claims have been made for vitamin E; that it improves sexual performance, increases fertility, and retards aging, but there is little satisfactory evidence to support any of these claims. Vitamin E's major role is as a natural antioxidant and, as such, it helps protect the cells from oxidative damage.

Function: As an antioxidant, vitamin E is thought to help protect against cancer and to boost the immune system, thus protecting against viral and bacterial infection. It prevents muscle inflammation and soreness after exercise, and may help treat arthritis and some skin conditions.

Deficiency: Unlikely, but research shows some evidence of muscle wasting and red blood cell damage when blood levels of Vitamin E are very low.

Risks: Very little risk of overdosing, but large doses may cause diarrhea.

Special needs: Pregant and lactating women, the elderly, people whose diet is high in polyunsaturated fats and oils. This is because these oils are easily oxidized, so the need for vitamin E is increased.

Main sources: Wheat germ, safflower, and sunflower oils, nut oils, olive oil, nuts, eggs, margarine, avocados.

Stability: Destroyed by exposure to air.

CALCIUM

RDA *Women and Men: 800-1200mg*

Calcium is the most abundant mineral in the body, wirh 99% found in the bones and teeth; the rest is in the blood and tissues. Bone mass peaks between the ages of 25 and 30, and then declines progressively. During and after the menopause, loss of bone mass accelerates rapidly.

Function: Strengthens the bones. Essential for nerve function, muscle contraction, enzyme activity, and blood clotting. Vitamin D promotes the absorption of calcium.

Deficiency: A deficiency will result in osteoporosis, and interferes with growth in children.

Risks: Unlikely, but may include

constipation or kidney stone formation, and can inhibit absorption of iron and zinc.

Special needs: Children, adolescents, pregnant and lactating women, and people with an inadequate vitamin D intake.

Main sources: Dairy products, fish, nuts, tofu, fruit, green leafy vegetables, sea vegetables.

MAGNESIUM

RDA *Women: 280mg Men: 350mg*

Magnesium is concentrated mainly in the bones and muscles, but it is also an essential part of all cells.

Function: Required for cell division, enzyme production, and muscle and nerve function. It is a component of bone and over 300 enzymes. Studies suggest that magnesium can lower blood pressure and may help alleviate asthma.

Deficiency: Thought to be rare and are likely to be a result of excessive losses through diarrhea rather than low intakes. Some nutritionists consider deficiencies to be more widespread than previously believed. Studies suggest that low levels of magnesium in the blood may be associated with increased risk of heart disease.

Risks: Unlikely.

Special needs: Pregnant and lactating women, alcoholics.

Main sources: Grains, nuts, pulses, vegetables, sea vegetables, fruits (particularly bananas).

IRON

RDA *Women: 15mg Men: 10mg*

The body contains 3-4 grams of iron, over half of which is in the form of hemoglobin, the red pigment in blood. Iron is also stored in the bone marrow, liver, and spleen. There are two types of iron - hem iron from meat and fish, and non-hem iron from vegetables and fortified foods. Hem iron is more easily absorbed than non-hem. Vitamin C promotes absorption of iron; tannin (in tea), oxalic acid (in spinach), and phytic acid (in grains) inhibit it.

Function: Needed for the production of red blood cells, transportation of oxygen around the body, and the functioning of enzymes. Deficiency: Iron deficiency causes anemia, one of the commonest deficiency diseases.

Risks: Ordinary supplementation can cause constipation, diarrhea, stomach pains. Very high doses can be toxic and even lethal. Toxic to people with hemochromatosis.

Special needs: Women with heavy periods, pregnant women, people suffering from iron-deficiency anemia.

Main sources: Red meat, liver, oysters, eggs, dried apricots, black strap molasses.

ZINC

RDA *Women: 12mg Men: 15mg*

The body contains about 2 grams of zinc, mostly found in muscle and bone. Zinc is not stored by the body so a daily intake is needed. Zinc from animal sources is usually much better absorbed than that from plant foods.

Function: Zinc regulates genetic material and the activities of an enormous number of enzymes. It reinforces the immune system and protects against infection. It is involved in the metabolism of protein, carbohydrates, and fats, the formation of bone tissue and healing of wounds. Zinc works as an antioxidant, and may help limit the spread of cancer.

Deficiency: The commonest symptoms of deficiency are skin problems, general fatigue, resistance to infections, loss of taste and appetite. During pregnancy, deficiency can result in the developmental disorder of the fetus.

Risks: High doses may cause nausea and vomiting. Long-term high doses may interfere with copper metabolism.

Special needs: After injury and surgical operations, pregnant and lactating women, growing children, the elderly, vegetarians, vegans.

Main sources: Meat, liver, poultry, seafood (especially oysters), eggs, milk, wheat germ, nuts, pulses, bread.

POTASSIUM

RDA *None. Average daily intake 2-4g.*

Potassium is among the minerals present in the largest quantity in the body. Almost all potassium is found in the fluid inside the cells. It is very easily excreted, especially if taking diuretic medicines, so a daily intake is essential. Higher intakes of potassium may counteract the effects of sodium (salt) and therefore reduce high blood pressure and the risk of stroke. Average adult intake should be 3.5 grams per day.

Function: Potassium is essential for the correct functioning of the heart, muscles, and nerves. It regulates fluid and mineral balance, and helps maintain normal blood pressure.

Deficiency: A deficiency can lead to fatigue, muscle weakness, bloating, constipation, cardiac arrhythmia, and insomnia.

Risks: Unlikely, since excess amounts are excreted, unless there is a problem with excretion.

Special needs: People who consume a lot of alcohol, coffee, sugar, and salty foods.

Main sources: Green vegetables, fruits (especially bananas), juices, dairy products, grains, coffee.

SELENIUM

RDA *Women: 55μg Men: 70μg*

Selenium is one of the trace elements in the soil which the body needs in very small amounts. The amount present in the soil varies from country to country. Selenium is part of an enzyme known as glutathione peroxidase, which is an antioxidant. This can help protect the cells against the harmful effects of oxidation.

Function: Selenium works as an antioxidant with vitamin E, and helps in cell growth. As an antioxidant, it protects against free radicals, and may help to prevent some cancers and heart disease.

Deficiency: A lack of selenium may increase the risk of heart disease and can cause Kaschin-Beck disease, which affects the cartilage in the joints.

Risks: High intakes have been reported to cause diseased nails, hair loss, and upset stomach.

Special needs: Young adults and elderly people, vegetarians, pregnant and lactating women, smokers, heavy drinkers.

Main sources: Nuts (especially brazil nuts), seeds, legumes, bread, fish, meat (especially pork), liver, kidney.

WATER

Although some foods contain a fair amount of water, it is also important to drink sufficient water. Experts suggest a consumption of 1-2 quarts every day.

COMMON NUTRITIONAL TERMS

Antioxidants

Protect the body by deactivating harmful substances known as free radicals. Widely believed to play a major role in protecting against coronary heart disease, some types of cancer, and possibly many other degenerative diseases. Natural antioxidants include vitamins C and E, carotenes, selenium, and zinc.

Cholesterol

Waxy substance naturally present in the cells and manufactured in the liver. Excess cholesterol in the blood can form fatty deposits that stick to the walls of the arteries. Excessive build-up restricts the flow of blood and oxygen to the brain and can thicken the blood, causing it to clot. Both factors can lead to heart disease and stroke. Also carries essential fatty acids around the blood stream and is involved in the production of vitamin D, various hormones, and bile salts that help digestion.

Diuretic

Food or drug that increases urine flow, thus helping to combat fluid retention. Asparagus and parsley are natural diuretics.

Enzymes

Proteins that act as catalysts, speeding up biological processes without being themselves involved.

Essential fatty acids

Polyunsaturated fatty acids which the body cannot make for itself. Two main categories are omega-3 and omega-6 (see page 15).

Free radicals

Aggressive molecules which can attack healthy cells, leaving them prone to disease. A certain number of free radicals can exist quite safely in the body, but damage may occur if their numbers increase. Environmental factors such as cigarette smoke, pesticides, polluted air, or even sunlight, which disturb the body's natural defense system, can cause an increase. It is believed that if free radicals attack DNA, the genetic material in the nucleus of a cell, the resulting changes may cause cancer.

Insoluble fiber

Type of fiber, such as cellulose, that cannot be broken down during its passage through the gut. Increases fecal bulk and helps prevent constipation and bowel disease.

Lipids

A collective term used to describe fats, oils, and waxes.

Lipoproteins

Low-density lipoproteins (LDLs) transport cholesterol around the bloodstream; high levels of LDLs are associated with high cholesterol levels, which increase risk of heart disease and stroke. High-density lipoproteins (HDLs) seem to lower the risk by returning surplus cholesterol to the liver for excretion.

Oxidation

Damage to cells caused by free radicals — similar to the type of reaction that causes an apple to go brown when exposed to the air.

Phytochemicals

Naturally occurring therapeutic compounds in fruits and vegetables that may help protect against cancer and heart disease. Examples include beta-carotene, indoles, and isothiocyanates.

Prostaglandins

Minute hormone-like substances present in body cells which stimulate bodily functions and secretions. Some types can activate inflammation and pain, or cause the blood to thicken; their action can be blocked with aspirin. Involved in the production of mucus which protects the stomach lining. Also stimulate contractions of the womb during childbirth.

Soluble fiber

Made up of pectins and gums found in foods such as oats, legumes, green vegetables, and dried fruits. Broken down by bacteria in the intestine, and known to help reduce high blood cholesterol levels.

Trace elements

Minerals present in the soil and sea. Amounts present in foods varies from area to area. needed by the body in tiny amounts. Examples include selenium, iodine, manganese, and copper.

Trans fatty acids

Type of unsaturated fatty acid created during the commercial hydrogenation or hardening of unsaturated oils. Occurring in meat and milk. They raise the level of "bad" cholesterol in the blood.

A holistic approach to cooking involves more than recipes and ingredients. The kitchen environment, hygiene, cookware, cooking techniques, and frame of mind when cooking all play their part in creating healing foods.

A HEALTHY KITCHEN

The kitchen is a favorite place for harmful bacteria. They multiply at an alarming rate in warm, moist conditions where there is food. Make sure your kitchen is scrupulously clean and dry, and you will keep them at bay.

- Disinfect worktops and keep them dry.
- Keep food covered and wipe up any spills.
- Make sure cooked food is cooled quickly and stored in the refrigerator.
- Keep a special chopping-board just for raw meats, poultry, and fish.
- Don't use the same knife for raw and cooked foods without washing it in between.
- Wash spoons between tastings to avoid introducing bacteria into the cooking pot.
- If you do the dishes by hand, use hot soapy water and rinse under running water.
- Change kitchen towels and thoroughly disinfect the sink daily.

Cookware

Pots and pans made from glass, ceramics, and earthenware are non-reactive and should be used to cook acidic foods such as tomatoes, lemons, wine, and vinegar. The best metal pots are made from high-gauge stainless steel, cast-iron, or enamel. Avoid aluminum since it sheds easily and is implicated in Alzheimer's disease. Heavy-based pots and pans distribute the heat evenly and prevent food from burning.

Nonstick cookware is essential if you are trying to reduce the fat in your diet, since you need only a minimum amount of oil, or none at all, to lubricate the food and prevent it from sticking. There is a wide choice available including skillets, sauté pans, ridged broiler pans, roasting, and cake pans.

A steamer and a pressure cooker are also useful for healthy cooking.

Getting organized

Before you start to cook, it is worth spending a little time getting organized. You can then relax and enjoy the actual process of preparing and cooking food.

- If you like to listen to music while you cook, choose something harmonious and soothing so you can concentrate on cooking.
- Read the recipe all the way through, then plan the sequence according to what needs marinating, soaking, chilling, etc.
- Have utensils and pans to hand.
- Make sure knives are sharp.
- Have all the ingredients ready and complete any preparation before cooking.
- Clear up as you go along, especially if you eat in the kitchen.

Cooking techniques

According to oriental healing traditions, the fuel used, cooking method, and temperature affect the healing properties of the food. Pressure cooking, stir-frying, and steaming are considered "balanced" techniques. At opposite ends of the spectrum are deep-frying and uncooked foods, which are respectively considered excessively yang (strong/heavy) and yin (weak/light). The

recommendation is to use a mixture of techniques according to the seasons and your own nutritional needs or those of the people for whom you are cooking.

Stir-frying is a flavorful and quick method of cooking even-sized pieces of food in a small amount of oil.

Wet-frying is a particularly healthy and fat-free technique for which you need a nonstick wok or skillet. Use 2 tablespoons of water, broth, or vegetable juice instead of oil, and use the same stirring and tossing technique as for stir-frying. The steam from the liquid is enough to cook the vegetables until they release their own juices.

Pressure cooking cuts the cooking time by at least half, and concentrates nutrients and juices. A pressure cooker is particularly useful if you are trying to increase your fiber intake. Dried peas, beans, and lentils do not need overnight soaking and cook in minutes. Tough meat cuts become meltingly tender.

Steaming is a fast and healthy alternative to boiling. Because the food does not come into contact with the cooking liquid, more vitamins are retained, although some are invariably lost through heat and others will leach into the cooking liquid. The liquid should always be retained and used in gravies and sauces or for cooking other foods. Steaming is especially good for vegetables since it preserves the texture and bright colors.

Broiling is a healthier option than frying when cooking meats, poultry, or fish. The food cooks in its own juices under intense heat, but will need to be marinated or brushed with oil or a sauce.

Vegetables

The World Health Organisation recommends that our daily intake, excluding potatoes, should be at least 1 pound. That means eating about five servings a day. Vegetables offer endless inspiration, consisting as they do of buds, leaves, stems, flowers, roots, and tubers, each with different culinary and therapeutic properties.

NUTRIENTS IN VEGETABLES

Together with fruits, vegetables are the most important source of fiber, vitamins, and minerals in the diet. They are one of the major sources of carotene (the plant form of vitamin A), vitamin C, and vitamin E. These vitamins collectively act as antioxidants, which protect against heart disease and some cancers. Vegetables also contain some of the B vitamins including folate, which is especially needed by growing children or if you're pregnant, or planning to get pregnant.

Vegetables provide essential minerals, particularly those needed by women: calcium to help prevent osteoporosis and iron to replace that lost in blood during menstruation.

RISKS

There are virtually no risks if washed and stored properly. A few vegetables contain natural toxins that could cause harm. For instance, potatoes contain small amounts of alkaloids which give them their characteristic taste. Greening, usually caused by exposure to light, indicates dangerously high alkaloid levels, as does sprouting. Throw away any potatoes with green spots or sprouting eyes. Cabbages contain goitogens, which may be a problem for those with goiter conditions. Celery can accumulate high levels of nitrates from the soil, which are potentially carcinogenic.

BUYING AND STORING

From the moment of harvest, vegetables begin to lose their nutrients. Warmth, wilting, and bruising activate enzymes which cause spoilage, and exposure to oxygen in the air causes large vitamin C losses. Leafy vegetables are particularly affected.

Because vegetables are one of the major sources of vitamins, it is essential to select only the freshest specimens and to store them correctly. Ideally, vegetables should be consumed on the day of purchase, but if your lifestyle does not permit a daily trip to the store, try to buy only enough for three to four days at a time.

Most vegetables will keep for a few days in a cool, dry, airy place. Root vegetables should be stored in the dark, otherwise they begin to sprout. Keep strong-smelling vegetables, such as onions and garlic, away from other food, and do not refrigerate them. Remove any close-fitting wrapping from prepacked vegetables, since this may cause them to sweat and subsequently rot.

PREPARING AND COOKING

Vitamin C and B vitamins are partially destroyed by heat, and they also leach into cooking water. Raw vegetables have the maximum fibre and nutrient content, with the exception of potatoes. For maximum nutritional benefit, it is helpful to bear in mind the following points:

❧ Eat vegetables raw, steam them, or cook them in water as briefly as possible, or stir-fry them in a tiny amount of oil. Microwave cooking retains the highest amount of water-soluble nutrients.

❧ Always save the cooking water and add it to other dishes.

❧ Peel or slice vegetables only when you are ready to use them; slicing tears the cells and releases an enzyme that hastens the oxidation of vitamin C.

❧ Tear salad leaves rather than chop them; this damages the cell less.

❧ Eat vegetables as soon as possible after preparation.

❧ Avoid reheating vegetables.

ASPARAGUS

Excellent source of beta-carotene, lutein, folate. Rich source of potassium. Useful source of vitamin C and E, thiamin (vitamin B1).

Asparagus is packed with antioxidants, folate, and potassium, which helps regulate cellular fluid. It is mildly laxative and contains the diuretic asparagine, which eliminates fluids and encourages urination. It is used in traditional healing to treat kidney problems.

Risks: Asparagus contains a group of organic compounds called purines. A high intake can lead to a build-up of uric acid salts, which can aggravate gout.

BEETS

Excellent source of potassium, folate.

Rich in complex carbohydrates, beetroot are a valuable source of energy and fiber. They are an excellent source of potassium and folate, one of the B vitamins needed for healthy cells. They also contain some vitamin C.

Risks: Beet greens are high in oxalic acid, and can inhibit calcium absorption if eaten to excess.

BELL PEPPERS

Excellent source of beta-carotene (red bell peppers), vitamin C. Useful source of potassium, niacin (vitamin B3), pyridoxine (B6).

Sweet or bell peppers, as they are usually known, start life as green and change to yellow and red as they ripen. The flavor becomes sweeter as they do so. Weight for weight, red bell peppers contain three times as much vitamin C as an orange. Bell peppers are an excellent source of beta-carotene; red peppers contain 20 times more than yellow ones. They also contain bioflavonoids which, together with beta-carotene and vitamin C, are antioxidants with cancer-fighting properties. Bell peppers contain a small amount of vitamin E, another antioxidant, and folate, one of the B vitamins, which builds healthy red blood cells.

BROCCOLI

Excellent source of potassium, beta-carotene, lutein, vitamin C. Good source of folate. Useful source of vitamin E.

Broccoli probably tops the list of disease-fighting vegetables. It is strongly indicated as having anti-cancer properties, particularly against breast, lung, and colon cancers. It is packed with carotenes, vitamin C, and vitamin E — all antioxidants which help protect against cancer. The darker the flowerets, the greater the concentration of vitamins. Like all cruciferous plants, broccoli contains phytochemicals which help prevent cancer-causing substances from damaging DNA, the genetic material in cells. Broccoli also contains B vitamins thiamin, niacin, and pyridoxine. Purple-sprouting broccoli is a rich source of calcium. Broccoli should be cooked very lightly in order to preserve the vitamin C content.

CABBAGE

Excellent source of vitamin C. Rich source of potassium, carotene. Good source of folate. Useful source of thiamin (vitamin B1).

Cabbage has been used by traditional healers for thousands of years to treat a wide range of complaints. Cabbage juice contains a substance called S-Methylmethionine, which is thought to have a healing action on the mucous membranes lining the gut. Modern research in the US, Greece, and Japan strongly suggests a link between regular cabbage consumption and a lower incidence of colon cancer. Cabbage also speeds up the metabolism of estrogen in women, which may help protect against breast and ovarian cancer. Cabbage needs to be cooked very lightly in order to preserve the vitamin content. Most of the nutrients are concentrated in the dark outer leaves.

CARROTS

Excellent source of beta-carotene, alphacarotene, lutein. Good source of potassium.

Carrots are nutritionally important as a major source of carotenes in the diet. As such, they are strongly implicated in protecting against certain cancers. Eating a single carrot a day is thought to reduce the risk of lung cancer by 50%. A daily carrot is also believed to improve night vision. Like all root vegetables, carrots contain energy-boosting starches and sugars, as well as fiber. Pectin, a soluble fiber, is believed to lower blood cholesterol levels. Carrots also contain vitamin C and some B vitamins.

CELERY

Rich source of potassium.

Having a high water content, celery is particularly low in calories and good to eat if you are trying to lose weight. It is also rich in potassium, which helps regulate blood pressure and fluid retention. For this reason, celery is used in traditional healing practice as a diuretic and to treat hypertension (high blood pressure). Scientists have discovered that it contains a compound called 3 n-butyl phthalide, which does lower blood pressure and also acts as a sedative. Herbalists use a tea brewed from celery seeds to treat gout.

CHILI PEPPERS

Excellent source of beta-carotene, potassium, vitamin C. Useful source of niacin (vitamin B3).

Weight for weight, fresh red chili peppers contain six times the beta-carotene and 13 times the vitamin C of a tomato. They also contain iron and B vitamins. Research suggests that chili peppers have a beneficial effect on the digestive system by increasing the secretion of saliva and gastric juices. They dilate the bronchial passages, clear the sinuses, and thin nasal mucus. Chili peppers also act as anticoagulants and may help lower blood pressure. Herbalists have long used cayenne (ground red chilies) as a heart, circulatory, and digestive stimulant. Being antibacterial and rich in vitamin C, cayenne is believed to help protect against colds and chills.

GARLIC

Excellent source of potassium. Useful source of pyridoxine (vitamin B6), vitamin C.

Garlic is renowned for its vast range of healing properties. Several studies have shown that the sulphurous compounds in garlic reduce blood pressure and blood cholesterol levels, inhibit blood clotting — thus reducing the risk of thrombosis — and may also help prevent the growth of malignant tumors. Studies have additionally shown that it inhibits the growth of harmful bacteria. As such, garlic is believed to have a powerful effect on wound healing. In the Indian system of Ayurvedic medicine, garlic is used to treat diarrhea and amebic dysentery, relieve bronchitis, flu, and asthma, and to expel intestinal parasites. If you are prepared to eat enough of it, garlic contains plenty of vitamins and minerals,

including magnesium, zinc, and the trace elements selenium and germanium. Both of these are thought to boost the immune system, and selenium has antioxidant properties similar to those of vitamins C and E.

KALE

Excellent source of potassium, beta-carotene, lutein, vitamin C. Rich source of folate. Useful source of calcium, vitamin E, pyridoxine (vitamin B6).

Overflowing with antioxidants and a wonderful source of chlorophyll, kale is a powerful anti-cancer agent. As with all cruciferous vegetables, kale is linked with lower incidences of colon, prostate, and bladder cancer. It is a useful source of calcium, needed for strong bones and teeth, and also contains reasonable amounts of magnesium and iron.

LETTUCE

Excellent source of beta-carotene, lutein. Good source of potassium. Useful source of folate.

Like all salad greens, lettuce is 90% water, but it still provides essential nutrients. The nutrients present depend on the variety, time of year, and state of freshness. Depending on the depth of color, lettuce is an excellent source of beta-carotene and another carotene called lutein, both of which are antioxidants which may help prevent cancer and heart disease. Carotenes are more concentrated in the dark-green outer leaves than in the paler inner leaves. Lettuce is also a useful source of folate — vital if you are pregnant since it may help prevent a number of birth defects. Lettuce also contains a small amount of thiamin (vitamin B1) and vitamin C.

Risks: Lettuce can accumulate high levels of nitrates from the soil, which are potentially carcinogenic. It should not be eaten in excessive amounts for long periods.

ONIONS

Useful source of potassium.

Like garlic, the strong sulphurous smell of onion juice led people to believe in its healing powers. In the Middle Ages in Europe, the onion was used as a talisman against the plague. It was commonly used to cure colds and disperse catarrh, and is still used by herbalists to treat warts and acne. Onion tea is used as a sedative. The onion is the subject of much modern scientific research. It appears that eating raw onions can reduce blood cholesterol levels, discourage blood clotting by thinning the blood, and break down clots once they have occurred, thus helping to prevent heart disease, thrombosis, and circulatory diseases. There is also some evidence that the sulphurous compounds in onions may inhibit the growth of cancer cells.

PARSLEY

Excellent source of potassium, beta-carotene, folate, vitamin C. Rich source of iron. Useful source of fiber, calcium, thiamin (vitamin B1).

Parsley is more than a garnish — it is a valuable source of nutrients if eaten in reasonable quantities. It can be made into a soup, a tea, or juice to help increase intake. Parsley contains far more vitamin C than citrus fruits, and is packed with beta-carotene — a cancer-fighting antioxidant. It is also an excellent source of folate, especially needed if you are pregnant, since it may help prevent birth defects. Parsley contains minerals vital for women: iron, zinc, and calcium, and is an excellent source of potassium which may help ease fluid retention. It is effective as a breath-freshener after eating garlic.

PEAS

Excellent source of lutein, thiamin (vitamin B1). Rich source of potassium, beta-carotene, vitamin C. Useful source of fiber, iron, niacin (vitamin B3), folate.

Peas are largely composed of sugars that turns to starch as peas ripen. Peas are a great source of energy and, unlike most vegetables, they contain a little protein. They contain useful amounts of pectin, a soluble fiber which helps lower blood cholesterol levels. A serving of peas provides half your daily thiamin requirement, needed for the release of energy from carbohydrates and for healthy nerve and muscle function. Peas contain plenty of vitamin C and beta-carotene — antioxidants that may help protect against cancer. They are also an excellent source of lutein, a carotene with anti-cancer properties similar to beta-carotene. Frozen peas contain fewer vitamins than fresh ones.

POTATOES

Excellent source of potassium. Useful source of thiamin (vitamin B1), pyridoxine (vitamin B6), folate, vitamin C.

Potatoes are a carbohydrate-rich food which provides us with fiber and some protein. However, their protein is considered incomplete since it is deficient in two essential amino-acids, methionine and cystine. Potatoes are an excellent source of potassium. Orange-fleshed sweet potatoes also contain plenty of beta-carotene, vitamin E, and vitamin C — antioxidants that may protect against cancer. Although they do not contain vast amounts of vitamin C, ordinary white-fleshed potatoes are a significant source because we eat them so often. Most of the vitamin C is concentrated in or close to the skins, so cook them unpeeled if possible. Potato skins are rich in chlorogenic acid, a polyphenol thought to prevent cell changes which lead to cancer. Potatoes also contain protease inhibitors, compounds which are known to combat certain carcinogens and viruses.

Risks: Green and sprouting potatoes contain dangerously high levels of alkaloids. They should be discarded.

PUMPKINS AND SQUASH

Excellent source of beta-carotene, alphacarotene, lutein. Useful source of potassium, vitamin C.

Pumpkins and varieties of squash, such as butternut or acorn, are a vital source of several types of carotene, which the body converts to vitamin A. Carotenes are antioxidants which may help protect the body from cancer, particularly lung cancer. Pumpkins and squash are especially important in a vegetarian diet, in which vitamin A from animal foods may be lacking. They are a carbohydrate- and fiber-rich food, which also contains magnesium, B vitamins, and vitamin E.

SPINACH

Excellent source of potassium, beta-carotene, lutein, folate Rich source of vitamin C. Useful source of calcium, magnesium, iron, vitamin E.

Spinach is one of the most nutrient-rich vegetables, containing vast amounts of carotenes which are strongly implicated in protecting against certain cancers, particularly lung cancer. Tests have also shown that carotenes can help prevent age-related macular degeneration, or deterioration of the retina, a common cause of blindness in elderly people. Spinach also contains large amounts of chlorophyll, another cancer-fighter. Contrary to popular belief, spinach is not a particularly rich source of iron, although it does contain useful amounts together with calcium and magnesium, and small amounts of zinc and B vitamins.

Risks: Spinach contains high levels of oxalic acid and should be eaten sparingly if you suffer from kidney stones.

WATERCRESS

Excellent source of beta-carotene, vitamin C. Good source of potassium. Useful source of calcium, iron, vitamin E, thiamin (vitamin B1), pyridoxine (vitamin B6).

Watercress contains large amounts of beta-carotene, vitamin C, and vitamin E — powerful antioxidants with cancer-fighting properties. A number of research studies have shown that a diet high in cruciferous vegetables is linked with lower incidences of cancers of the colon, rectum, and bladder. Watercress is a natural antibiotic and has long been used in traditional medicine to treat kidney problems, jaundice, sore throats, respiratory problems, and skin complaints.

Risks: Watercress grown in the wild should not be eaten since it may contain a parasite known as the liver fluke, which, as the name suggests, attacks the liver. Wild watercress can also be contaminated with the bacteria that causes listeria. Even cultivated watercress should always be washed in several changes of water.

Fruits

Fruits are among the most convenient and readily available foods. Most varieties need no cooking and can be prepared with minimum effort.

Fruits contain a range of nutrients vital to good health. The World Health Organization recommends eating at least five servings of fruits or vegetables a day, so we need to develop the habit of snacking on fruits and to use them more often as part of a meal.

NUTRIENTS IN FRUITS

Fruits and fresh fruit juices are the major provider of vitamin C in the diet. However, the content varies quite widely depending on the type of fruit, and some of the vitamin will always be lost during cooking. The commonest source is citrus fruits (oranges, lemons, limes, and grapefruit), but guavas, strawberries, kiwifruit, papaya, and mangoes, are also excellent sources.

Orange-fleshed fruits such as mangoes and orange-fleshed melons are packed with beta-carotene, the plant form of vitamin A. Dried apricots are another particularly rich source. Carotenes such as alpha-carotene, lutein, and lycopene are found in red- and orange-fleshed fruit. Carotenes act as antioxidants, which are thought to protect against damage to the cells by free radicals.

It is important to eat plenty of fruits since they also provide essential bulk and fiber for the digestive system. Many varieties contain pectin, a type of soluble fiber thought to help lower blood cholesterol levels. A few examples include apples, apricots, blackcurrants, and figs.

Fruits contain a very small amount of protein, no fat, and very few calories, being composed mostly of water. However, densely-fleshed fruits, such as bananas, grapes, mangoes, and most dried fruits, contain useful amounts of carbohydrates, and are good for boosting energy levels.

Some fruit varieties are particularly rich in potassium, which helps to regulate blood pressure, and all are low in sodium — a good nutritional balance. Fruits also contain calcium, magnesium, iron, folate, pyridoxine (vitamin B6), selenium, and a small amount of zinc. Some fruits contain other B vitamins and vitamin E.

RISKS

Because it is assumed that people do not eat citrus fruit peel, this is invariably coated with fungicides to prevent mold growth. However, the finely grated zest (the colored outer layer of peel) of lemons, limes, and oranges gives a wonderfully refreshing tangy flavor to all types of dishes. If you like to use citrus zest in cooking, or if you make marmalade, it is wise to use unwaxed fruit. Otherwise, throughly scrub the fruit under warm running water. Apple pips are poisonous because of their amygdalin content. Swallowing one occasionally is not a hazard.

STORING FRUITS

From the moment of harvest, fruits begin to lose their nutritional value and flavor. Fully ripened fruits should be eaten within a day or two of purchase. Otherwise, store them in the salad drawer of the refrigerator (except bananas, which will turn black), or in a cool, airy store-room in winter. Store unripe fruits at room temperature.

PREPARING FRUITS

To make the most of the vitamins in fruits, they are best eaten raw, because vitamins are partially destroyed by cooking. However, sharp-tasting fruits such as rhubarb, acerola, and tamarillos need cooking to make them palatable, so bear in mind the following points in order to make the most of the nutrients:

♠ Wash fruits quickly — soaking leaches nutrients into the water.

♠ Avoid peeling unless absolutely necessary — nutrients are often concentrated just below the skin, and the skin provides fiber.

♠ Prepare fruits just before you cook them — exposing cut surfaces to the air destroys nutrients by oxidation.

♠ Use minimum water for stewing and cook for the shortest possible time. Keep the juice to serve with the fruit.

APPLES

Useful source of carbohydrates, fiber, and vitamin C.
Apples are a good source of fructose, a natural sugar which helps stabilize blood sugar levels. Apples contain pectin, a soluble fiber thought to lower blood cholesterol. One study suggests that pectin might also help prevent colon cancer. In herbal medicine, grated raw apple is used to stop diarrhea — the pectin it contains helps solidify the feces.

APRICOTS

Excellent source of beta-carotene. Rich source of potassium, fiber (dried apricots), iron (dried). Useful source of carbohydrates (dried), magnesium (dried).
Apricots are packed with beta-carotene, the plant form of vitamin A. Because of this, apricots are thought to help prevent certain cancers, notably those related to smoking. Compared with fresh apricots, dried fruits are far richer in nutrients and also in calories. They make a handy snack and are one of the best health foods available.
Risks: The sulfur dioxide used to preserve the color of dried apricots may trigger an asthma attack in sensitive people.

BANANAS

Excellent source of potassium. Good source of vitamin C. Useful source of pyridoxine (vitamin B6). Source of magnesium.
Bananas contain high levels of slow-release carbohydrates, which boost energy levels. They are a favorite with athletes and sustaining when you are burning up a lot of energy. They are also one of the best sources of potassium. Being bland and slightly sweet, bananas are sometimes a comfort food for children.

BLUEBERRIES AND BILBERRIES

Rich source of beta-carotene, vitamin C.
Blueberries have always been used by herbalists to treat diarrhea and urinary infections such as cystitis. In Sweden, soup made from the closely-related bilberry, native to Scandinavia, is used to treat childhood diarrhea. Medical research now shows that the tannins and anthocyanosides in blueberries and bilberries are indeed bactericidal and antiviral, and are used to treat irritations of the throat, mouth, and gums, as well as diarrhea. Studies in Paris and Budapest suggest that the same substances may also protect against hardening of the arteries. Pecarin, made from powdered bilberry skins, is an antidiarrheal drug now made in Sweden and exported.

CHERRIES

Rich source of potassium. Useful source of vitamin C and E.
Cherries have always been valued for their cleansing properties, and are believed to flush out toxins and excess fluid, and cleanse the kidneys. Cherries contain ellagic acid, thought to fight cancer by blocking an enzyme used by cancer cells. Cherries are also mildly laxative and can help alleviate constipation.

CRANBERRIES

Useful source of vitamin C.
Folk medicine has always used cranberry juice for treating chronic urinary tract and bladder infections such as cystitis. Medical studies both in the United States and Israel are now showing positive results. Although it was once thought that cranberries worked by increasing the acid in the urine and thus destroying harmful bacteria, it now appears that that the berries contain a substance which stops bacteria clinging to the cells that line the urinary tract and bladder. Even so, cranberries really only help prevent urinary infections. Once the infection has taken hold, antibiotics are usually needed.

FIGS

Excellent source of potassium (fresh and dried). Rich source of fiber (dried). Good source of calcium (dried). Useful source of magnesium (dried), iron (dried).
Figs have been used medicinally for thousands of years and are widely used in traditional healing as a poultice for boils, in water as a gargle for sore throats, and as an anti-cancer agent. Japanese research now shows that figs contain a therapeutic substance called benzaldehyde, which has proved to be effective in reducing malignant tumors. Scientists have also isolated enzymes in figs which are thought to aid digestion. Dried figs are a much more concentrated source of nutrients than fresh figs. They are exceptionally rich in pectin, a soluble fiber that helps lower blood cholesterol levels, and in cellulose, an insoluble fiber which assists the passage of food through the gut. Syrup of figs is a traditional remedy for constipation.
Risks: Dried figs, as with all dried fruits, are high in sugars and so may cause tooth decay if eaten too often.

GRAPEFRUIT

Excellent source of vitamin C, beta-carotene (pink grapefuit), lycopene (pink grapefruit). Good source of potassium.

Grapefruit, especially pink-fleshed varieties, are packed with vitamin C and beta-carotene. Studies have shown that the pectin in the flesh and fibrous membrane may contain potent substances that lower blood cholesterol and could possibly reverse the effects of atherosclerosis (clogging of the arteries). Studies in Sweden and the Netherlands suggest that the bioflavonoids in grapefuit (and other citrus fruits) may help reduce the risk of certain cancers.

GRAPES

Good source of potassium. Source of beta-carotene, vitamin C, and phosphorus.

Grapes are one of the oldest and delicious fruits known. Grapes are thirst-quenching and easy to digest, which is perhaps why they are traditionally offered to invalids. Red and black grapes are high in bioflavonoids — antioxidants thought to neutralize free radicals — and so may help protect against cancer and heart disease. They are rich in tannins, which are thought to be antiviral.

Risks: Unwashed grape skins are likely to be contaminated with dust, yeasts, fungicides, and pesticide residues. Red grapes may trigger migraines in susceptible people.

GUAVAS

Excellent source of beta-carotene, lycopene, vitamin C, potassium.

Similar in size to a small apple, guavas have a yellow-green skin and creamy, strongly-scented flesh. They are packed with vitamin C, containing five times more than an orange. Despite losses through heat, canned guavas are still an excellent source of vitamin C. Guavas are also exceptionally rich in beta-carotene and lycopene (another type of carotene), both of which act as antioxidants and neutralize cell damage from free radicals. Guavas also contain pectin, a soluble fiber which helps lower blood cholesterol levels.

KIWIFRUITS

Excellent source of vitamin C. Good source of potassium.

Originally known as the Chinese gooseberry after its country of origin, kiwifruits are commonly used in Chinese medicine to treat stomach and breast cancer. A single kiwifruit provides more than the daily adult requirement of vitamin C. Kiwifruit also provides pectin, a soluble fiber which helps lower blood cholesterol levels.

LEMONS AND LIMES

Excellent source of vitamin C. Good source of potassium.

Lemons and limes stimulate the appetite and aid digestion. In traditional healing, lemons are used to heal sores and insect bites, and to soften corns. The Romans believed lemons were the antidote to all poisons — a belief borne out by modern studies which have shown that lemon juice poured over shellfish destroys most of the harmful bacteria. A slice of lime or lemon in a mug of hot water is a wonderfully cleansing drink first thing in the morning. Like all citrus fruits, lemons and limes provide valuable amounts of vitamin C. They are rich in bioflavonoids which act like antioxidants, helping to protect the body against free radicals.

MANGOES

Excellent source of beta-carotene, vitamin C. Good source of potassium.

In traditional healing practice, mangoes are believed to have a calming, energy-producing action and are used to treat nervous indigestion. A single serving of mango contains 7 grams of fiber, which makes it a highly effective laxative. Mangoes are packed with beta-carotene and vitamin C, which act as antioxidants, protecting against cancer and heart disease.

MELONS

Excellent source of beta-carotene and lycopene. Rich source of vitamin C. Good source of potassium.

Melons have been used in folklore the world over to treat diverse conditions ranging from hepatitis (jaundice) and worms to menstrual problems and cancer. They are considered cooling and therefore used to alleviate "hot" digestive problems such as dyspepsia, stomach ulcers, acidity, and colitis. All melons are rich in vitamin C, while orange-fleshed varieties are exceptionally high in beta-carotene, an antioxidant which helps protect against cancer and heart disease. Green- and yellow-fleshed melons contain very little carotene. Watermelons contain massive amounts of lycopene, another type of carotene, which may help to protect against various cancers.

ORANGES

Excellent source of vitamin C. Good source of potassium.

One orange supplies more than the daily adult requirement of vitamin C, which helps fight infection and is one of the antioxidants that may protect against cancer. Several studies have shown a link between regularly eating plenty of oranges and lower incidences of certain cancers. Other studies show that the pectin present in the flesh and membrane of oranges and other citrus fruits can lower blood cholesterol levels and protect the arteries. The membranes also contain bioflavonoids, which have antioxidant properties.

PAPAYAS

Excellent source of beta-carotene, vitamin C. Rich source of potassium.

One of the most luscious fruits with velvety sweet flesh, a single papaya will provide over twice the daily amount of vitamin C and more than enough beta-carotene — both natural antioxidants which help protect against cancer and heart disease. Papayas also provide small amounts of calcium and iron. They contain an enzyme called papain which breaks down protein and aids digestion. The enzyme is also used commercially as a meat tenderizer.

PEACHES

Rich source of vitamin C, betacarotene. Good source of potassium.

Peaches are one of the most sensual of fruits. They are easy to digest and mildly laxative. Eaten unpeeled, they provide almost all your daily vitamin C requirement. Canned peaches have lost more than 80% of their vitamin C. Like most orange-fleshed fruits, yellow peaches contain beta-carotene — a natural antioxidant that helps protect against cancer and heart disease. The nutrients in dried peaches are much more concentrated. They are an excellent source of beta-carotene, potassium, and niacin (vitamin B3), and are rich in iron.

PEARS

Good source of potassium.

Pears are high in the natural sugars fructose and glucose, making them a convenient source of energy. They are also a source of soluble and insoluble fiber, which respectively help lower blood cholesterol levels and ease the passage of food through the gut. They contain some vitamin C, which is concentrated in the skin.

PINEAPPLES

Good source of potassium. Useful source of vitamin C.

Pineapple is believed to alleviate anxiety, to calm digestion, cool a fever, and to soothe inflammations both inside and outside the body. Gargling with pineapple juice was a traditional remedy for sore throats. It seems that there is scientific evidence to back up these claims. Pineapples contain a digestive enzyme called bromelain, which is prescribed in tablet form to people with digestion problems, and as an anti-inflammatory agent to treat arthritis. There is also some evidence that bromelain may help dissolve blood clots, and it is therefore useful in treating heart disease. It may also help with sinus congestion and urinary infections.

Risks: Bromelain may cause dermatitis.

PLUMS AND PRUNES

Plums are a rich source of potassium, beta-carotene. Prunes are a useful source of iron, beta-carotene, niacin (vitamin B3), and pyridoxine (vitamin B6).

Plums contain vitamin E which, together with beta-carotene, is a natural antioxidant which may help protect against cell damage caused by free radicals. Prunes, the dried variety of plums, contain copious amounts of pectin which accounts for their laxative effect. They are also a more concentrated source of potassium than plums.

RASPBERRIES

Excellent source of vitamin C. Good source of potassium.

Raspberries contain vitamin E, folate (one of the B vitamins), and fiber, and a bowlful will provide all the vitamin C you need for a day. Raspberries are used extensively in traditional healing, particularly to treat frequent urination. Tea made from the leaves has been used for centuries to treat the female reproductive system. Recent tests on animals have even shown that the unripe fruit has an estrogen-like effect. Drinking the tea in the last three months of pregnancy is known to alleviate labor pains and make delivery easier. The tea also helps with period pain, and can be used to treat mild digestion problems.

STRAWBERRIES

Excellent source of vitamin C. Good source of potassium.

Weight for weight, strawberries contain more vitamin C than citrus fruits. Strawberries are a good source of pectin, a form of soluble fiber, and lignin, a non-soluble fiber found in the tiny seeds that dot the surface. In folklore, they were credited with curative powers and were used to eliminate kidney stones, alleviate gout and rheumatism, and to whiten the teeth and skin with the juice. In oriental medicine, they are considered moistening and are used for sore throats, hoarseness, and for cleansing the blood.

Risks: Strawberries are often implicated in food allergies, and may cause swellings, upset stomach, and hayfever-like reactions in susceptible people.

Grains

Grains contain the plant's embryo, and with it a package of concentrated nutrients to support the new plant growth. No wonder, then, that grains have a quality or life force unequaled by most other foods. Grains were one of the first foods that could be stored for long periods, and for this reason they form the staple diet for most of the world's population. Without them there would be no bread, no pasta, no cakes or cookies, and no breakfast cereals.

NUTRIENTS IN GRAINS

Grains provide us with the complex carbohydrates and a small amount of fat essential for maintaining energy levels; 3½ ounces of grains provides 300-400 calories and 2-6 grams of fat.

Beneath the indigestible husk which covers most grains lies an outer protective layer of bran which is the major source of fiber in the diet. Beneath this lies the starchy endosperm, which makes up most of the grain. The endosperm contains a storehouse of carbohydrates and protein to support the growing plant, and provides us with energy and amino-acids needed for the growth and repair of cells. At the heart of the endosperm lies the embryo or germ, from which the new plant grows. It is rich in enzymes, protein, minerals, fats, and vitamins.

Many grains contain useful amounts of magnesium, needed for healthy muscles and cells, and iron, needed to prevent anemia and to carry oxygen around the blood. Grains are also a valuable source of B vitamins, needed mainly for the release of energy from carbohydrates and fats.

For maximum nutritional benefit, use whole grains with the bran still intact. They are much richer in fiber and contain higher levels of most B vitamins, iron, protein, and vitamin E.

RISKS

The phytic acid present in some grains may interfere with the absorption of calcium and iron. Excess bran can irritate the bowel. Barley, oats, rye, and wheat contain gluten — a mixture of cereal proteins — which needs to be avoided by people suffering from celiac disease.

BUYING AND STORING

For a better flavor and texture, choose grains that have been subjected to minimal processing. Old-fashioned rolled oats are better for you than quick-cooking oats; ordinary coarse-ground cornmeal has more nutrients and flavor than instant cornmeal.

Keep your grains in an airtight container in a cool, dark, dry place; exposure to heat, air, and light turns them rancid.

Because they contain the germ and the bran, whole grains have a higher fat content and therefore a much shorter shelf life than refined grains. Whole grains like bulgur wheat, that have been cracked or ground, thus exposing the germ to the air, have an even shorter shelf-life. Buy them in small amounts and store in a cool place or in the refrigerator. They will last for 4-5 months before turning rancid. Refined or polished grains, such as white rice, can be stored for up to a year.

PREPARING AND COOKING

Before soaking or cooking, pick over the grains and remove any foreign bodies. Put the grains in a pan and cover with plenty of water. Swish the water thoroughly with your fingers and then drain. Repeat this process four or five times, until the water is more or less clear. There is no need to wash risotto rice since it is the surface starch which gives a risotto its creamy texture. Polished rice should also not be washed since it has a protein- and vitamin-enriched coating.

Grains expand to two to four times their size during cooking, so choose a saucepan that will allow for this. A heavy-based pan is best for slow-cooked dishes, since it prevents them scorching. Grains are usually cooked in water, but a light broth, diluted tomato juice, or the water from cooked vegetables have more flavor. The amount of liquid required depends on the age of the grain and how soft or firm you like the cooked grain to be. A good guide with rice and many other grains is to cover with water to the depth of your thumbnail.

AMARANTH

Excellent source of iron. Good source of protein, calcium. Useful source of fiber, carbohydrates.

Amaranth is high in lysine, one of the vital amino-acids commonly lacking in grains. Combined with a low lysine grain such as wheat, it provides good-quality protein.

BARLEY

Rich source of fiber. Useful source of protein, carbohydrates.

One of the most ancient cultivated grains, barley is a useful source of carbohydrates but contains few vitamins. In folk medicine, it is called the "medicine of the heart," and is also used to treat constipation. It is rich in soluble and insoluble fiber which respectively lower blood cholesterol, thus reducing the risk of heart disease, and ease the passage of food through the gut.

BUCKWHEAT

Good source of potassium, magnesium, thiamin (vitamin B1), niacin (vitamin B3), pyridoxine (vitamin B6). Useful source of protein, carbohydrates, iron.

Buckwheat is rich in lysine, a vital amino-acid, and is wheat-free. It contains a small amount of selenium, a trace mineral thought to protect against cancer and boost the immune system.

CORNMEAL

Good source of potassium, thiamin (vitamin B1). Useful source of protein, carbohydrates.

Cornmeal, also called grits, maize flour, and polenta, is made from ground corn kernels. It is less nutritious than wheat but contains small amounts of magnesium, iron, zinc, and niacin (vitamin B3). It is gluten-free. Blue cornmeal contains more protein and iron than yellow or white varieties.

MILLET

Excellent source of thiamin (vitamin B1), iron, potassium. Rich source of magnesium. Useful source of protein, carbohydrates, riboflavin (vitamin B2), niacin (vitamin B3), zinc.

A particularly nutritious grain containing high levels of a wide range of nutrients. It is gluten-free and useful for people suffering from celiac disease. In European folk medicine, millet has a reputation for strengthening the nails and hair if eaten three times a week.

OATS

Excellent source of potassium, thiamin (vitamin B1). Good source of magnesium, iron, zinc. Useful source of protein, carbohydrates, fiber, vitamin E, and niacin (vitamin B3).

Oats are one of the most valuable of grains, containing high levels of nutrients. They contain slightly more fat than other grains and therefore turn rancid more quickly. Oats are particularly valued for their ability to dramatically lower blood cholesterol levels. They work as a laxative by increasing fecal bulk. In traditional healing, oats are thought to raise the energy and general vitality, which may be why they are used as a breakfast food. Herbalists and homeopaths use oats to treat stress-related exhaustion.

QUINOA

Good source of protein. Useful source of carbohydrates, fiber, calcium, iron, vitamin E, thiamin (vitamin B1), niacin (vitamin B3), iron, zinc, magnesium.

An ancient grain of the Incas, quinoa is one of the best grain-based sources of protein, calcium, and iron. It is also a useful source of vitamin E, an antioxidant which neutralizes cell damage from free radicals. It may help prevent cancer.

RICE (BROWN)

Excellent source of thiamin (vitamin B1), niacin (vitamin B3). Good source of magnesium. Useful source of carbohydrates, potassium, zinc, vitamin E, folate.

Brown rice contains a wide range of vitamins and minerals, including small amounts of protein, fiber, and iron. Even though phytic acid partially inhibits absorption of calcium and iron, brown rice is a better source of B vitamins, minerals, and protein than white rice. Rice has long been used to treat kidney problems, diabetes, and severe blood pressure. Studies have shown that it stabilizes blood sugar and insulin levels, and may prevent kidney stones from forming.

WHEAT

Excellent source of potassium, thiamine (vitamin B1). Useful source of protein, carbohydrates, fiber, iron, zinc, niacin (vitamin B3), folate.

Whole wheat contains a wide variety of valuable nutrients, whereas refined wheat provides mainly carbohydrates and few vitamins and minerals. Wheat is classified as hard or soft, depending on gluten content. Durum wheat, the hardest, is used to make pasta; strong wheat flour is used in bread-making; and low-gluten flours are used for cakes and pastries. Whole-wheat flour is a useful source of B vitamins and fiber. Semolina, also known as cream of wheat, consists of coarse particles ground from the endosperm, and is used to make couscous and desserts. Bulgur wheat is cracked, steamed, and roasted, during which some of the bran is lost. Wheat bran is one of the best cures for constipation. Numerous studies indicate that eating high-fiber foods, including wheat bran, is linked to lower rates of colon cancer.

Dried lentils, peas, and beans (pulses)

Dried lentils, peas, and beans (pulses or legumes), are among the most important foods in the diet, and feature in cuisines around the world.

NUTRIENTS

Pulses are an important source of slow-release complex carbohydrates. Because the starches in pulses are digested slowly, they release a steady stream of glucose into the bloodstream. For this reason, they are useful in controlling insulin levels in diabetes. They are good news for dieters — most contain only a trace of fat and between 80 and 110 calories after cooking.

Pulses are extremely high in pectin — the soluble fiber which helps lower blood cholesterol levels. A 3-ounce serving per day is thought to reduce cholesterol by 10%. Pulses contain insoluble fiber too, and this increases the bulk of the faeces, easing the passage of food through the gut and possibly reducing the risk of bowel cancer.

Pulses are rich in most of the B vitamins, needed for the release of energy from carbohydrates, but they are lacking in vitamin B12, essential for the production of red blood cells. They contain valuable amounts of calcium, iron, folate, magnesium, zinc, and potassium too. Eating beans with vitamin C-rich foods such as chili peppers, bell peppers, tomatoes, or in a salad with citrus fruits, helps increase iron absorption.

Sprouted pulses such as mung bean sprouts are much lower in calories and fat, and are an excellent source of vitamin C and enzymes.

For vegetarians, pulses are an essential part of the diet since they contain plenty of protein. However, all pulses except soybeans lack some of the essential amino-acids in protein which the body needs. Grains, nuts, and dairy products make up the missing-amino acids, so combining these with pulses will produce the same sort of protein that you would get by eating meat. Dairy products will also make up for the lack of vitamin B12 referred to earlier.

Pulses are notorious for causing unwelcome flatulence. It is caused by oligosaccharides — sugar molecules bonded together in such a way that digestive enzymes cannot break them down. Therefore, the bacteria present in the large intestine take on this role, giving off various gases in the process, and this results in flatulence. Lengthening the soaking or cooking time is recommended, as well as adding fennel or dill to the cooking water. A product called "Beano" can also be added to decrease gas production.

Soybeans contain a substance called a trypsin-inhibitor which prevents the body from absorbing protein. To remove this, the beans should be boiled for at least one hour.

Do not cook pulses in a slow-cooker or microwave oven, since the temperature will never be high enough to destroy the toxins.

BUYING AND STORING

Pulses tend to toughen with age, so buy them in small quantities. If you are buying pulses loose, check them for unwanted debris, and discard any that are wrinkled or split. Store for up to 9-12 months in airtight containers away from sunlight.

PREPARATION AND COOKING

Lentils do not need soaking because of their flat shape and small size, but dried beans, peas, and chickpeas do; the exact time depends on type and age. Their weight will approximately double during soaking and cooking. Soak in cold water overnight, but if you are short of time you can cover them with boiling water and soak for 2-3 hours. Always drain and cover with fresh water before cooking. Do not add salt to the cooking water until the last 10 minutes of cooking time. If added earlier, salt toughens the skins and makes them indigestible.

ADUKI BEANS

Excellent source of potassium, zinc. Rich source of thiamin (vitamin B1). Good source of protein, carbohydrates, fiber, magnesium, niacin (vitamin B3). Useful source of iron.

These tiny sweet-flavored beans are probably the most digestible of all beans. In Japan they are known as the "King of Beans" because they are so nutritious. They are a great source of important minerals such as potassium, zinc, magnesium, and iron, and they contain some calcium too. Aduki beans are an ingredient in oriental confectionery.

BLACK BEANS (BLACK TURTLE BEAN)

Excellent source of thiamin (vitamin B1). Rich source of protein, potassium, magnesium, folate, iron, calcium. Good source of carbohydrates, fiber. Useful source of niacin (vitamin B3).

These earthy-flavored beans have a high thiamin content and are particularly rich in folate. They contain plenty of minerals, including small amounts of selenium, a trace element which may help protect against cancer, heart disease, and the toxic effects of environmental pollutants.

CHICKPEAS

Excellent source of potassium, folate. Good source of protein, carbohydrates, fiber, magnesium, iron, zinc, thiamin (vitamin B1). Useful source of calcium, vitamin E, riboflavin (vitamin B2), niacin (vitamin B3).

Deliciously nutty and comforting, chickpeas are one of the easiest pulses to digest. They are the main ingredient in hummus, the well-known Middle Eastern dip. Chickpeas contain more iron, zinc, riboflavin, and vitamin E than most pulses. They also contain manganese; animal studies have shown that a deficiency in this mineral may impair fertility.

KIDNEY BEANS

Excellent source of thiamin (vitamin B1). Rich source of potassium, magnesium, folate. Good source of protein, carbohydrates, fiber. Useful source of iron, niacin (vitamin B3).

Kidney beans have a rich, floury texture and are the essential bean in Chilli con Carne and Frijoles Refritos. Compared with other varieties, they are a particularly rich source of potassium, magnesium, and folate. Kidney beans also contain small amounts of calcium and selenium, a trace element thought to protect against cancer and heart disease. They have a diuretic action and are used in oriental healing to treat fluid retention.

LENTILS (GREEN AND BROWN)

Excellent source of iron, pyridoxine (vitamin B6). Rich source of potassium, zinc, thiamin (vitamin B1), folate. Good source of protein, carbohydrates, fiber, magnesium, selenium. Useful source of riboflavin (vitamin B2), niacin (vitamin B3).

Together with rice, lentils are the staple food in India where they are known as "dhal." They are easy to digest and quick to prepare. Packed with minerals, B vitamins, and fiber, compared with other pulses they contain much more iron, zinc, and folate. Lentils also contain pyridoxine, a B vitamin needed for healthy nerves, skin, muscle, and blood.

MUNG BEANS

Excellent source of potassium. Rich source of magnesium, zinc, thiamin (vitamin B1), folate. Good source of protein, carbohydrates, fiber, iron. Useful source of riboflavin (vitamin B2), niacin (vitamin B3), pantothenic acid (vitamin B5), pyridoxine (vitamin B6).

These small green beans are also sold as beansprouts. They are particularly rich in potassium, magnesium, zinc, and B vitamins, and contain more fiber and iron than most pulses.

NAVY BEANS

Excellent source of potassium. Rich source of magnesium, thiamin (vitamin B1). Good source of protein, carbohydrates, fiber, iron, zinc, pyridoxine (vitamin B6). Useful source of calcium.

Also known as Great Northern, Boston, or Haricot beans, these small white beans are the principal ingredient in canned baked beans. They readily absorb other flavous and are good in slow-cooked casseroles. They contain more fiber, iron, and zinc than most other pulses.

SOYBEANS

Excellent source of protein, potassium, magnesium, thiamin (vitamin B1), folate. Rich source of iron, zinc. Good source of carbohydrates, fiber, calcium, vitamin E. Useful source of riboflavin (vitamin B2), niacin (vitamin B3), pyridoxine (vitamin B6).

The soybean is called the "beef" of China, not only because of its high protein content but also because the protein is similar to that of animal foods, since it is complete in all the essential amino-acids. Soybeans contain far more minerals, carbohydrates, B vitamins, and vitamin E than any other bean, and they are also a concentrated source of essential fatty acids (including omega-3 normally found in oily fish). Recent research shows that soybeans contain isoflavones, a weak form of the female hormone estrogen, which may lower the risk of heart disease, prostate, and breast cancer and osteoporosis. Eating 2 ounces of beans a day may also decrease the symptoms of the menopause.

Meat, poultry, and game

MEAT

The nutritional benefits of meat should not be overlooked. Provided it is eaten sparingly, meat can contribute to a healthy diet.

Nutrients in meat

Meat is an invaluable source of high quality protein which contains all the amino-acids needed by the body. It is a major provider of B vitamins, including vitamin B12 — likely to be lacking in a vegan diet. Meat also provides important minerals.

Risks

High intakes of meat, poultry, and game are linked to colon cancer. Saturated fats in meat can be a conributing factor in causing heart disease.

Buying and storing

Since ill health arising from meat consumption may be caused by the cocktail of chemicals and type of food given to the animals, it is safest to choose organically-reared meat. Choose extra-lean ground meats and lean cuts for kabobs and stir-fries. Store meat loosely covered in the refrigerator making sure that it does not drip onto other foods.

Preparing and cooking

There are several ways to reduce your fat intake from meat: trim off all visible fat; roast or broil on a rack to let any fat drain away; drain off any fatty liquid that appears when cooking ground meat. The healthiest cooking methods are broiling, stir-frying, and "wet-frying" (see page 119).

BEEF

Excellent source of potassium; niacin (vitamin B3), vitamin B12. Rich source of zinc. Good source of protein, pyridoxine (vitamin B6). Useful source of iron, vitamin E, phosphorus. 3½ ounces of trimmed lean beef provides around 135 calories and 5 g fat.

Beef is a major supplier of B vitamins, although it contains only very small amounts of folate. It is a source of essential trace elements — selenium, iodine, chromium, and silicon — which the body needs in very small amounts.

LAMB

Excellent source of potassium, niacin (vitamin B3), vitamin B12. Good source of protein, zinc, pyridoxine (vitamin B6). Useful source of riboflavin (vitamin B2). 3½ ounces of trimmed lean lamb provides around 155 calories and 8 g fat.

As with all meat, lamb is a particularly good source of niacin and vitamin B12. The fat content varies depending on cut.

PORK

Excellent source of potassium, niacin (vitamin B3), vitamin B12. Good source of protein. Useful source of zinc, riboflavin (vitamin B2). 3½ ounces of trimmed lean pork provides around 125 calories and 4 g fat.

The lean cuts of pork are lower in fat than beef or lamb. It is a major source of B vitamins and zinc, and contains small amounts of magnesium and selenium, a valuable trace element thought to help prevent cancer and heart disease.

POULTRY

With the trend towards eating less red meat, we are eating more poultry than ever before.

Nutrients in poultry

Poultry is a valuable source of protein, B vitamins, and some minerals — particularly potassium, iron, and zinc. The fat content of the white meat of chicken, especially without the skin, is lower than that of red meat, and the fatty acids are mainly unsaturated and do not raise blood cholesterol levels.

Risks

There is a risk of food poisoning from undercooked chicken.

Buying and storing

Choose good-quality, free-range birds. Poultry deteriorates rapidly so make sure it is fresh with no bad smells. Store loosely covered in the refrigerator for up to 2 days, making sure it does not drip onto other food.

Cooking

Steaming, broiling, and stir-frying are the healthiest methods.

CHICKEN

Excellent source of potassium, niacin (vitamin B3). Good source of protein, vitamin B12. Useful source of pyridoxine (vitamin B6). 3½ ounces of skinless chicken provides around 105 calories and 2 g fat.

Without the skin, chicken is particularly lean. The brown meat contains significantly more fat that the white meat. It is not so rich in B vitamins and minerals as meat but it does contain small amounts of magnesium, zinc, iron, selenium, thiamin (vitamin B1), and riboflavin (vitamin B2).

DUCK

Excellent source of niacin (vitamin B3), vitamin B12. Rich source of potassium. Good source of protein, riboflavin (vitamin B2). Useful source of iron, zinc. 3½ ounces of skinless duck provides around 135 calories and 7 g fat.

Removing the skin greatly reduces the fat content of duck. Duck contains over twice the thiamin and riboflavin of chicken as well as more iron and zinc, so it is worth eating on a few occasions. Barbary ducks have a better flavor and more flesh than ordinary varieties of duck.

TURKEY

Excellent source of potassium, niacin (vitamin B3), vitamin B12. Good source of protein. Useful source of zinc, riboflavin (vitamin B2). 3½ ounces of skinless turkey provides around 105 calories and 2 g fat.

Turkeys are becoming readily available all the year round, and are an excellent choice of low-fat meat. Turkeys are a major source of most B vitamins, particularly vitamin B12 and thiamin, but contain very little folate. They contain small amounts of magnesium as well as selenium, an important trace element thought to protect against cancer.

GAME

Game is becoming more widely available to meet the need for a chemical-free alternative to meat and poultry.

Nutrients in game

Wild game has had endless exercise in its search for food, so the flesh will be lean and muscular without the build-up of fat reserves present in ordinary meat. Farmed game will be slightly less lean. The fat in game is mainly the unsaturated type that does not raise blood cholesterol levels. It is a valuable source of protein and richer in B vitamins and iron than ordinary meat.

Risks

Lead shot may be embedded in the flesh of wild game.

Buying and storing

Game should not smell rotten or putrid even if it has been hung. Store it losely covered in the refrigerator, making sure that it does not drip onto other food.

Preparing and cooking

Game meat often needs to be marinated to tenderize it. Young, tender game can be roasted or broiled. Older game is better cooked by moister methods such as braising.

PHEASANT

Excellent source of potassium, niacin (vitamin B3), vitamin B12 Rich source of protein. Good source of pyridoxine (vitamin B6). Useful source of iron, zinc, riboflavin (vitamin B2). 3½ ounces of dressed pheasant provides around 115 calories and 6 g fat.

Pheasant is usually dressed to counteract dryness, and this can raise the fat content, but it is still relatively lean. Like all game birds, pheasant is an excellent source of B vitamins, and contains more iron and zinc than chicken.

PIGEON

Excellent source of potassium, riboflavin (vitamin B2), niacin (vitamin B3), vitamin B12. Rich source of protein, iron, pyridoxine (vitamin B6). Useful source of zinc. 3½ ounces of dressed pigeon provides around 185 calories and 8 g fat.

Pigeon is richly-flavored, with dense, dark red flesh. It is an excellent source of many of the B vitamins, and a particularly rich source of iron and protein. It contains a useful amount of zinc and some magnesium and selenium.

RABBIT

Excellent source of potassium, niacin (vitamin B3), vitamin B12. Rich source of riboflavin (vitamin B2). Good source of protein. Useful source of zinc. 3½ ounces of rabbit provides around 135 calories and 6 g fat.

Rabbit, farmed or wild, has a pleasant, relatively delicate flavor and deserves to be used more often in cooking. Rabbit is low in fat and a valuable source of most B vitamins. It also contains small amounts of magnesium, iron, and selenium.

VENISON

Excellent source of potassium, niacin (vitamin B3) and vitamin B12. Good source of protein, zinc, pyridoxine (vitamin B6), vitamin B12. Useful source of iron, riboflavin (vitamin B2). 3½ ounces of venison haunch provides around 100 calories and 2 g fat.

Amazingly low in fat, venison contains particularly high levels of potassium, zinc, and iron, and small amounts of magnesium and selenium.

Fish and seafood

Fish and seafood are tremendously versatile, simple to cook, and easily digested.

NUTRIENTS IN FISH AND SEAFOOD

All fish and seafood are a valuable source of the high-quality protein needed for the maintenance and repair of body cells.

They provide us with a wide variety of essential minerals, especially phosphorus which is essential for strong bones, and potassium, needed for nerve and muscle function and to regulate blood pressure.

Together with sea vegetables (see page 62), marine fish are the richest source of iodine in the diet — needed for the production of thyroid hormones which help to control metabolism. Fish and seafood also contain selenium, a trace element which may help protect against cancer, heart disease, toxicity from heavy metals, and auto-immune deficiency.

Small fish, such as sardines and sprats, and canned salmon, have soft, edible bones which are a handy source of calcium, needed for healthy bones and teeth.

Oily fish are one of the few dietary sources of vitamin D, needed for calcium absorption. All fish and seafood are an important source of B vitamins, especially the essential vitamin B12, found principally in animal foods and necessary for red blood cell formation. Compared with other foods, they contain more pyridoxine — a valuable B vitamin needed for protein metabolism and a healthy nervous system.

Fish contains less fat than meat and, being high in unsaturated fatty acids, what fat there is happens to be the healthy kind. In oily fish, such as mackerel and herring, the fat is dispersed throughout the flesh, with a content between 10 and 20%. In white fish, such as halibut, sea bass, snapper, and cod, the fat is stored in the liver, so the amount in the flesh can be as low as 0.5%.

Fish oils play an increasingly vital role in the diet. They contain two essential fatty acids — eicosapentanoeic acid (EPA) and docosahexaenoic acid (DHA). Together, these form part of a group of fatty acids known as the omega-3 series, which are thought to offer protection from heart disease. EPA, in particular, produces a hormone-like substance called prostaglandin 3. This is known to reduce blood cholesterol levels and to reduce the risk of blood clots which can lead to thrombosis and stroke. Current research shows that fish oils can be useful in treating diabetes, skin disease, and rheumatoid arthritis, and are essential for the development of the eyes and brain.

RISKS

Shellfish and mollusks may harbor harmful bacteria, and should be thoroughly cooked. Make sure oysters for eating raw come from a pure source. Some people are sensitive to shellfish and may develop an allergic reaction to eating them.

Freshwater fish from lakes in industrial areas may be contaminated with heavy metals and other pollutants.

White fish, such as cod, must be thoroughly cooked to destroy parasitic worms and their eggs.

BUYING AND STORING

Fish should smell pleasant with no strong fishy odors. The skin will be shiny and wet-looking, the flesh springs back when lightly pressed, the gills are moist and reddish-pink, and the eyes clear and bulging. Fish should be taken home immediately after purchase, and unpacked and gutted before storing in the coldest part of the refrigerator. Cook fish within 24 hours of purchase.

PREPARING AND COOKING

Simple cooking methods such as steaming, stir-frying, and broiling are the best ways to bring out the flavor of fish and preserve essential nutrients. Poaching and simmering are good for white fish. All fish tends to toughen when overcooked, so keep cooking times to a minimum. Fish is cooked when the flesh has just turned opaque; if cooking a whole fish, check the meatiest part along the backbone.

Before cooking mussels, discard any that do not close when tapped with a knife. After cooking, discard any that have not opened.

COD AND HADDOCK

Excellent source of potassium. Good source of protein, vitamin B12. Useful source of niacin (vitamin B3). 3½ ounces of cod or haddock provides around 80 calories and less than 1 gram of fat.

All white fish store their fat in the liver, leaving the flesh almost fat-free. The liver is extremely rich in vitamins A and D, but the flesh contains few of the minerals and B vitamins found in oily fish. Even so, white fish is a good source of vitamin B12 and contains iodine and selenium.

MACKEREL

Excellent source of vitamin B12. Rich source of potassium. Good source of protein, vitamin D. Useful source of thiamin (vitamin B1), riboflavin (vitamin B2), pyridoxine (vitamin B6). 3½ ounces of mackerel provides around 220 calories and 16 grams of fat.

Mackerel is improved by sharp-tasting sauces and broiling under fierce heat to burn off excess oil. It is one of the most nutritious of oily fish, packed with B vitamins, including over five times the normal daily requirement of vitamin B12. It is a great source of omega-3 essental fatty acids.

MUSSELS

Excellent source of vitamin B12. Rich source of potassium, iron. Good source of zinc. Useful source of protein, riboflavin (vitamin B2), niacin (vitamin B3), folate. 3½ ounces of mussels provides around 75 calories and 2 grams of fat.

Mussels are an extremely valuable source of B vitamins and minerals, and are low in fat. They are relatively high in sodium, providing well over half the daily requirement. In oriental medicine, mussels are thought to strengthen the life force or *chi* and are used to treat goiter; this may be linked to their high iodine content.

OYSTERS

Excellent source of zinc, vitamin B12. Rich source of potassium, iron. Useful source of protein, calcium, thiamin (vitamin B1), niacin (vitamin B3), pyridoxine (vitamin B6). 3½ ounces of oysters provides around 65 calories and 1 gram of fat.

Oysters are a concentrated powerhouse of nutrients. Of all the foods, they are the richest source of zinc, containing nearly ten times the recommended daily amount. Zinc is thought to help protect against prostate cancer.

SALMON AND TROUT

Excellent source of potassium, niacin (vitamin B3), vitamin B12. Rich source of vitamin D, pyridoxine (vitamin B6). Good source of protein. Useful source of vitamin E, thiamin (vitamin B1). 3½ ounces of salmon provides around 180 calories and 11 grams of fat.

Both are rich in protein, minerals, vitamins, and omega-3 fatty acids common to all oily fish. Pacific salmon is a useful source of retinol, which the body converts to vitamin A. Atlantic salmon contains very little.

SARDINES

Excellent source of potassium, vitamin D, niacin (vitamin B3), vitamin B12. Good source of protein. Useful source of riboflavin (vitamin B2), pyridoxine (vitamin B6). 3½ ounces of sardines provide around 165 calories and 9 grams of fat.

Fresh sardines are ideal for barbecuing, while canned sardines make a nutritious snack as well as tasty dips and sandwich fillings. Sardines are one of the least expensive of oily fish. They are high in vitamin D and niacin. Bones in canned sardines provide calcium.

SHRIMP

Excellent source of potassium, vitamin B12. Good source of protein, vitamin E. Useful source of zinc. 3½ ounces of shrimp provides around 75 calories and less than 1 gram of fat.

Shrimp contain more protein than fish and are very low in fat. They are also a very good source of vitamin E, providing about half the average daily intake. They also contain small amounts of calcium, magnesium, iron, selenium, iodine, and riboflavin. Shrimp are high in cholesterol.

SQUID

Excellent source of pantothenic acid (vitamin B5), vitamin B12. Rich source of potassium, pyridoxine (vitamin B6). Useful source of protein, vitamin E. 3½ ounces of squid provides around 80 calories and just under 2 grams of fat.

The firm meaty flesh of squid needs only the briefest cooking. It is unusually rich in pantothenic acid, a B vitamin needed for cell growth and the production of essential fatty acids. Squid contains vitamin E — an antioxidant which helps to protect against cell damage by free radicals. It is also extremely high in cholesterol, but there is some evidence that this does not affect blood cholesterol levels.

TUNA

Excellent source of potassium, niacin (vitamin B3), vitamin B12. Rich source of iron, vitamin D. Good source of protein. Useful source of pyridoxine (vitamin B6). 3½ ounces provides 135 calories and 5 grams of fat.

Tuna is a major source of B vitamins and omega-3 fatty acids. Canned or fresh, tuna contains over twice the average daily requirement of niacin — far more than any other fish. The dark flesh contains nearly seven times more iron than the white flesh.

Nutritional Analysis
of the Recipes

18 LEMON HERB TEA

per portion serving 2

Kilocalories	less than 1
Kilojoules	2
Carbohydrate	negligible
Fat	negligible
Percentage of total calories from fat	negligible

18 GINGER AND MINT TEA

per portion serving 2

Kilocalories	5
Kilojoules	21
Protein	negligible
Carbohydrate	1g
Fat	negligible
Percentage of total calories from fat	negligible

20 WHEATFLAKE BARS WITH BANANAS AND FRESH ORANGE JUICE

per portion serving 1

Kilocalories	384
Kilojoules	1634
Protein	10g
Carbohydrate	87g
Dietary Fiber	12g

Good source of calcium, magnesium, potassium, iron, zinc, iodine, thiamin, riboflavin, niacin. vitamin B6, C & E

Fat	2g
of which saturates	less than 1g
of which monounsaturates	less than 1g
of which polyunsaturates	less than 1g
Percentage of total calories from fat	4%
of which saturates	less than 1%

18 HOT PEAR JUICE WITH CARDAMON

per portion serving 2

Kilocalories	5
Kilojoules	21
Protein	negligible
Carbohydrate	1g
Dietary Fiber	negligible

Good source of iron

Fat	less than 1g
of which saturates	less than 1g
of which monounsaturates	less than 1g
of which polyunsaturates	less than 1g
Percentage of total calories from fat	18%
of which saturates	0

22 WARM DRIED FRUIT COMPÔTE WITH SWEET COUSCOUS

per portion serving 4

Kilocalories	282
Kilojoules	1198
Protein	6g
Carbohydrate	64g
Dietary Fiber	7g

Good source of calcium, potassium, iron, iodine, niacin,

Fat	2g
of which saturates	less than 1
of which monounsaturates	less than 1
of which polyunsaturates	less than 1
Percentage of total calories from fat	6%
of which saturates	2%

20 TOASTED NUT GRANOLA IN FRUIT JUICE

per portion serving 12

Kilocalories	339
Kilojoules	1431
Protein	8g
Carbohydrate	51g
Dietary Fiber	5g

Good source of magnesium, iron, zinc, thiamin, niacin, vitamin B6, C & E

Fat	13g
of which saturates	4g
of which monounsaturates	2g
of which polyunsaturates	2g
Percentage of total calories from fat	34%
of which saturates	11%

22 BUCKWHEAT PANCAKES

per portion serving 20

Kilocalories	47
Kilojoules	198
Protein	2g
Carbohydrate	8g
Dietary Fiber	less than 1g

Good source of potassium

Fat	1g
of which saturates	less than 1g
of which monounsaturates	less than 1g
of which polyunsaturates	less than 1g
Percentage of total calories from fat	21%
of which saturates	4%

24 SMOKED TOFU KEDGEREE WITH ALMONDS

per portion serving 6

Kilocalories	282
Kilojoules	1184
Protein	12g
Carbohydrate	31g
Dietary Fiber	1g

Good source of calcium, potassium, iron, zinc, iodine, thiamin, riboflavin, niacin, vitamin B12, folate & E

Fat	13g
of which saturates	3g
of which monounsaturates	6g
of which polyunsaturates	3g
Percentage of total calories from fat	41%
of which saturates	9%

30 BLACK BEAN AND ROASTED TOMATO SOUP

per portion serving 4

Kilocalories	172
Kilojoules	729
Protein	12g
Carbohydrate	23g
Dietary Fiber	1g

Good source of calcium, magnesium, iron, zinc, thiamin, riboflavin, niacin, vitamin B6, folate, C & E.

Fat	4g
of which saturates	less than 1g
of which monounsaturates	2g
of which polyunsaturates	less than 1g
Percentage of total calories from fat	20%
of which saturates	3%

34 TOMATO AND PUMPKIN SEED BREAD

per portion serving 12

Kilocalories	257
Kilojoules	1088
Protein	9g
Carbohydrate	47g
Dietary Fiber	3g

Good source of potassium, iron, zinc, selenium, thiamin, niacin, vitamin B6, folate.

Fat	5g
of which saturates	less than 1g
of which monounsaturates	2g
of which polyunsaturates	2g
Percentage of total calories from fat	18%
of which saturates	3%

28 MISO SOUP WITH RICE NOODLES AND VEGETABLES

per portion serving 4

Kilocalories	116
Kilojoules	487
Protein	3g
Carbohydrate	22g
Dietary Fiber	2g

Good source of potassium, iron, thiamin, niacin, vitamin B6, folate, A & C.

Fat	1g
of which saturates	less than 1g
of which monounsaturates	less than 1g
of which polyunsaturates	less than 1g
Percentage of total calories from fat	12%
of which saturates	2%

32 BROCCOLI AND PINE NUT FRITTATA WITH ROASTED PEPPER SAUCE

per portion serving 6

Kilocalories	250
Kilojoules	1204
Protein	15g
Carbohydrate	8g
Dietary Fiber	3g

Good source of calcium, potassium, iron, zinc, iodine, thiamin, riboflavin, niacin, vitamin B6, B12, folate, A, C & E.

Fat	22g
of which saturates	8g
of which monounsaturates	8g
of which polyunsaturates	5g
Percentage of total calories from fat	69%
of which saturates	24%

36 EGGPLANT, ARTICHOKE AND TOMATO PHYLLO TART

per portion serving 6

Kilocalories	266
Kilojoules	1112
Protein	9g
Carbohydrate	17g
Dietary Fiber	2g

Good source of calcium, potassium, iron, selenium, thiamin, riboflavin, niacin, vitamin B6, B12, folate, A, C & E.

Fat	19g
of which saturates	5g
of which monounsaturates	11g
of which polyunsaturates	2g
Percentage of total calories from fat	63%
of which saturates	18%

28 CARROT AND CORIANDER SOUP

per portion serving 6

Kilocalories	96
Kilojoules	401
Protein	2g
Carbohydrate	15g
Dietary Fiber	3g

Good source of potassium, thiamin, niacin, vitamin B6, folate A & C.

Fat	4g
of which saturates	2g
of which monounsaturates	less than 1g
of which polyunsaturates	less than 1g
Percentage of total calories from fat	36%
of which saturates	22%

34 WARM BUTTERNUT SQUASH SALAD

per portion serving 4

Kilocalories	348
Kilojoules	1448
Protein	7g
Carbohydrate	24g
Dietary Fiber	7g

Good source of calcium, magnesium, potassium, iron, zinc, thiamin, niacin, vitamin B6, folate, A, C & E.

Fat	25g
of which saturates	4g
of which monounsaturates	15g
of which polyunsaturates	4g
Percentage of total calories from fat	65%
of which saturates	9%

40 CHOCOLATE, CRANBERRY, AND WALNUT MUFFINS

per portion serving 12

Kilocalories	170
Kilojoules	715
Protein	5g
Carbohydrate	20g
Dietary Fiber	3g

Good source of potassium, iron, zinc, selenium, thiamin, niacin, vitamin B6, B12, folate.

Fat	9g
of which saturates	3g
of which monounsaturates	2g
of which polyunsaturates	3g
Percentage of total calories from fat	46%
of which saturates	18%

40 LEMON RICE CAKE

per portion serving 16

Kilocalories	143
Kilojoules	602
Protein	6g
Carbohydrate	17g
Dietary Fiber	less than 1g

Good source of calcium, potassium, iodine, riboflavin, niacin, vitamin B6, B12, folate & E.

Fat	6g
of which saturates	9g
of which monounsaturates	3g
of which polyunsaturates	1g
Percentage of total calories from fat	39%
of which saturates	9%

42 OLIVE OIL, SESAME, AND HONEY CAKE

per portion serving 16

Kilocalories	318
Kilojoules	1321
Protein	6g
Carbohydrate	20g
Dietary Fiber	2g

Good source of iron, zinc, thiamin, riboflavin, niacin, vitamin B6, B12, & E

Fat	24g
of which saturates	4g
of which monounsaturates	16g
of which polyunsaturates	4g
Percentage of total calories from fat	69%
of which saturates	10%

44 YOGURT, BANANA, AND DRIED APRICOT SHAKE

per portion serving 2

Kilocalories	159
Kilojoules	672
Protein	7g
Carbohydrate	32g
Dietary Fiber	3g

Good source of calcium, potassium, iron, riboflavin, niacin, vitamin B6, B12, folate and C

Fat	1g
of which saturates	less than 1g
of which monounsaturates	less than 1g
of which polyunsaturates	less than 1g
Percentage of total calories from fat	7%
of which saturates	4%

44 KIWIFRUIT AND STRAWBERRY PIGNOLIA

per portion serving 3

Kilocalories	320
Kilojoules	1338
Protein	7g
Carbohydrate	39g
Dietary Fiber	4g

Good source of magnesium, potassium, iron, thiamin, riboflavin, niacin, vitamin B6, folate, C & E.

Fat	16g
of which saturates	2g
of which monounsaturates	4g
of which polyunsaturates	8g
Percentage of total calories from fat	45%
of which saturates	7%

48 ROASTED EGGPLANT AND PEPPERS WITH CORIANDER CREAM

per portion serving 4

Kilocalories	171
Kilojoules	712
Protein	4g
Carbohydrate	8g
Dietary Fiber	3g

Good source of calcium, potassium, iron, riboflavin, niacin, vitamin B6, folate A, C & E.

Fat	14g
of which saturates	6g
of which monounsaturates	6g
of which polyunsaturates	1g
Percentage of total calories from fat	75%
of which saturates	30%

48 PAPAYA AND SNOW PEA SALAD WITH LIME AND PISTACHIO DRESSING

per portion serving 4

Kilocalories	249
Kilojoules	1031
Protein	4g
Carbohydrate	8g
Dietary Fiber	3g

Good source of potassium, iron, thiamin, niacin, vitamin B6, folate, A, C & E.

Fat	23g
of which saturates	3g
of which monounsaturates	5g
of which polyunsaturates	13g
Percentage of total calories from fat	82%
of which saturates	48%

50 CHICKPEA CRÊPES WITH BLACK BEAN, CARROT, AND MANGO SALAD

per portion serving 6

Kilocalories	258
Kilojoules	1078
Protein	9g
Carbohydrate	24g
Dietary Fiber	5g

Good source of potassium, iron, zinc, thiamin, riboflavin, niacin, vitamin B6, folate, A, C & E.

Fat	15g
of which saturates	2g
of which monounsaturates	7g
of which polyunsaturates	4g
Percentage of total calories from fat	51%
of which saturates	7%

52 PECAN RICE , RADISH, AND RADICCHIO WITH GRIDDLED SHRIMP

per portion serving 4

Kilocalories	125
Kilojoules	519
Protein	14g
Carbohydrate	2g
Dietary Fiber	1g

Good source of potassium, iron, zinc, selenium, iodine, niacin, vitamin B12, folate, C & E.

Fat	7g
of which saturates	1g
of which monounsaturates	4g
of which polyunsaturates	1g
Percentage of total calories from fat	50%
of which saturates	7%

52 PINK GRAPEFRUIT, AVOCADO, AND WALNUTS WITH MIXED LEAVES

per portion serving 4

Kilocalories	190
Kilojoules	785
Protein	3g
Carbohydrate	4g
Dietary Fiber	3g

Good source of potassium, iron, thiamin, riboflavin, niacin, vitamin B6, folate, A, C & E.

Fat	18g
of which saturates	3g
of which monounsaturates	8g
of which polyunsaturates	6g
Percentage of total calories from fat	84%
of which saturates	12%

56 RED CABBAGE ROULADES WITH WILD RICE AND NUT STUFFING

per portion serving 6

Kilocalories	225
Kilojoules	935
Protein	4g
Carbohydrate	10g
Dietary Fiber	1g

Good source of calcium, potassium, niacin, vitamin B6 & E.

Fat	19g
of which saturates	5g
of which monounsaturates	10g
of which polyunsaturates	3g
Percentage of total calories from fat	75%
of which saturates	19%

58 SEA VEGETABLE AND SHIITAKE STIR-FRY WITH BROWN RICE

per portion serving 4

Kilocalories	240
Kilojoules	1008
Protein	5g
Carbohydrate	36g
Dietary Fiber	8g

Good source of calcium, magnesium, potassium, iron, zinc, iodine, thiamin, niacin, vitamin B6, B12, folate & C.

Fat	9g
of which saturates	1g
of which monounsaturates	2g
of which polyunsaturates	5g
Percentage of total calories from fat	35%
of which saturates	5%

58 SEA VEGETABLE, CARROT, AND SNOW PEAS WITH RICE NOODLES

per portion serving 4

Kilocalories	225
Kilojoules	937
Protein	4g
Carbohydrate	36g
Dietary Fiber	6g

Good source of potassium, iron, iodine, thiamin, niacin, vitamin B6, B12, folate, A, C & E.

Fat	7g
of which saturates	1g
of which monounsaturates	3g
of which polyunsaturates	2g
Percentage of total calories from fat	27%
of which saturates	55%

60 ASIAN RATATOUILLE WITH GINGERED RICE

per portion serving 6

Kilocalories	502
Kilojoules	2068
Protein	10g
Carbohydrate	75g
Dietary Fiber	3g

Good source of potassium, iron, zinc, thiamin, riboflavin, niacin, vitamin B6, folate, A, C & E.

Fat	19g
of which saturates	3g
of which monounsaturates	10g
of which polyunsaturates	4g
Percentage of total calories from fat	34%
of which saturates	6%

62 BLACK BEAN, SQUASH, AND ROOT VEGETABLE CASSEROLE

per portion serving 6

Kilocalories	249
Kilojoules	1048
Protein	11g
Carbohydrate	39g
Dietary Fiber	7g

Good source of calcium, magnesium, potassium, iron, zinc, thiamin, riboflavin, niacin, vitamin B6, folate, A, C & E.

Fat	6g
of which saturates	1g
of which monounsaturates	3g
of which polyunsaturates	1g
Percentage of total calories from fat	23%
of which saturates	3%

62 GREENS AND BEANS WITH PASTA AND GARLIC CHIVES

per portion serving 6

Kilocalories	357
Kilojoules	1470
Protein	13g
Carbohydrate	45g
Dietary Fiber	8g

Good source of calcium, magnesium, potassium, iron, zinc, selenium, thiamin, riboflavin, niacin, vitamin B6, folate, A, C, & E.

Fat	13g
of which saturates	4g
of which monounsaturates	5g
of which polyunsaturates	2g
Percentage of total calories from fat	34%
of which saturates	11%

66 MIXED SEAFOOD RICE

per portion serving 6

Kilocalories	347
Kilojoules	1466
Protein	24g
Carbohydrate	48g
Dietary Fiber	2g

Good source of potassium, iron, zinc, selenium, iodine, thiamin, riboflavin, niacin, vitamin B6, B12, folate A, C & E.

Fat	8g
of which saturates	1g
of which monounsaturates	4g
of which polyunsaturates	1g
Percentage of total calories from fat	21%
of which saturates	3%

68 SEARED TUNA WITH ASIAN GREENS

per portion serving 4

Kilocalories	391
Kilojoules	1632
Protein	48g
Carbohydrate	9g
Dietary Fiber	7g

Good source of calcium, magnesium, potassium, iron, zinc, selenium, iodine, thiamin, riboflavin, niacin, vitamin B6, B12, folate, A, C & E.

Fat	18g
of which saturates	4g
of which monounsaturates	7g
of which polyunsaturates	6g
Percentage of total calories from fat	42%
of which saturates	9%

68 ORIENTAL STEAMED SNAPPER

per portion serving 4

Kilocalories	222
Kilojoules	932
Protein	32g
Carbohydrate	2g
Dietary Fiber	1g

Good source of potassium, iron, selenium, iodine, thiamin, riboflavin, niacin, vitamin B6 & B12.

Fat	9g
of which saturates	2g
of which monounsaturates	3g
of which polyunsaturates	12g
Percentage of total calories from fat	37%
of which saturates	7%

70 TROUT FILLETS WITH PASSION FRUIT SAUCE

per portion serving 4	
Kilocalories	281
Kilojoules	1173
Protein	36g
Carbohydrate	3g
Dietary Fiber	1g

Good source of potassium, iron, selenium, and niacin.

Fat	14g
of which saturates	3g
of which monounsaturates	3g
of which polyunsaturates	less than 1g
Percentage of total calories from fat	45%
of which saturates	10%

76 SPICED LAMB AND APRICOT KABOBS

per portion serving 4	
Kilocalories	408
Kilojoules	1708
Protein	27g
Carbohydrate	38g
Dietary Fiber	5g

Good source of calcium, potassium, iron, thiamin, niacin, vitamin B6, B12 and folate.

Fat	18g
of which saturates	1g
of which monounsaturates	6g
of which polyunsaturates	1g
Percentage of total calories from fat	39%
of which saturates	3%

80 VENISON CASSEROLE WITH RED WINE, ORANGE, AND ROSEMARY

per portion serving 8	
Kilocalories	336
Kilojoules	1414
Protein	35g
Carbohydrate	22g
Dietary Fiber	7g

Good source of calcium, magnesium, potassium, iron, zinc, selenium, thiamin, riboflavin, niacin, vitamin B6, folate, A, C & E.

Fat	10g
of which saturates	2g
of which monounsaturates	6g
of which polyunsaturates	1g
Percentage of total·calories from fat	26g
of which saturates	6%

70 FISH KABOBS WITH COCONUT AND CORIANDER SAUCE

per portion serving 4	
Kilocalories	390
Kilojoules	1625
Protein	38g
Carbohydrate	5g
Dietary Fiber	less than 1g

Good source of calcium, magnesium, potassium, iron, zinc, selenium, iodine, thiamin, riboflavin, niacin, vitamin B6, B12, A & C.

Fat	25g
of which saturates	8g
of which monounsaturates	10g
of which polyunsaturates	4g
Percentage of total calories from fat	58%
of which saturates	19%

78 CHICKEN FAJITAS

per portion serving 4	
Kilocalories	265
Kilojoules	1157
Protein	25g
Carbohydrate	28g
Dietary Fiber	2g

Good source of potassium, iron, zinc, selenium, iodine, thiamin, riboflavin, niacin, vitamin B6, B12, folate, A, C & E.

Fat	7g
of which saturates	1g
of which monounsaturates	3g
of which polyunsaturates	2g
Percentage of total calories from fat	23%
of which saturates	4%

84 STIR-FRY OF YELLOW PEPPERS, ZUCCHINI AND TOMATOES

per portion serving 4	
Kilocalories	112
Kilojoules	470
Protein	4g
Carbohydrate	11g
Dietary Fiber	3g

Good source of potassium, iron, thiamin, niacin, vitamin B6, folate, A, C & E.

Fat	6g
of which saturates	1g
of which monounsaturates	4g
of which polyunsaturates	1g
Percentage of total calories from fat	51%
of which saturates	8%

74 BROILED PEPPERED CHICKEN WITH THYME-LIME PESTO

per portion serving 4	
Kilocalories	555
Kilojoules	2309
Protein	38g
Carbohydrate	2g
Dietary Fiber	1g

Good source of calcium, potassium, iron, zinc, selenium, iodine, thiamin, riboflavin, niacin, vitamin B6, B12, folate and E.

Fat	44g
of which saturates	8g
of which monounsaturates	27g
of which polyunsaturates	6g
Percentage of total calories from fat	72%
of which saturates	14%

78 BEEF STIR-FRY WITH EGGPLANT AND BROCCOLI

per portion serving 4	
Kilocalories	237
Kilojoules	993
Protein	24g
Carbohydrate	10g
Dietary Fiber	4g

Good source of potassium, iron, niacin, vitamin B6, B12, folate, A, C & E.

Fat	12g
of which saturates	12g
of which monounsaturates	5g
of which polyunsaturates	3g
Percentage of total calories from fat	45%
of which saturates	12%

84 BROCCOLI, CARROTS AND SUGAR SNAP PEAS WITH LEMON ZEST, AND OLIVE OIL

per portion serving 4	
Kilocalories	96
Kilojoules	398
Protein	6g
Carbohydrate	10g
Dietary Fiber	5g

Good source of potassium, thiamin, niacin, vitamin B6, folate, A, C & E.

Fat	4g
of which saturates	1g
of which monounsaturates	2g
of which polyunsaturates	1g
Percentage of total calories from fat	37%
of which saturates	6%

86 SESAME ROASTED ROOTS

per portion serving 6

Kilocalories	257
Kilojoules	1105
Protein	7g
Carbohydrate	44g
Dietary Fiber	9g

Good source of calcium, magnesium, potassium, iron, thiamin, niacin, vitamin B6, folate, A, C & E.

Fat	8g
of which saturates	1g
of which monounsaturates	5g
of which polyunsaturates	1g
Percentage of total calories from fat	26%
of which saturates	4%

86 GARLIC-ROASTED POTATOES WITH ROSEMARY AND OLIVES

per portion serving 4

Kilocalories	292
Kilojoules	1227
Protein	6g
Carbohydrate	48g
Dietary Fiber	3g

Good source of potassium, iron, thiamin, niacin, vitamin B6, folate and C.

Fat	10g
of which saturates	1g
of which monounsaturates	6g
of which polyunsaturates	1g
Percentage of total calories from fat	29%
of which saturates	4%

88 ALGERIAN CARROTS

per portion serving 4

Kilocalories	105
Kilojoules	434
Protein	1g
Carbohydrate	12g
Dietary Fiber	3g

Good source of potassium, iron, thiamin, folate, vitamin A, C & E.

Fat	6 g
of which saturates	1g
of which monounsaturates	4g
of which polyunsaturates	1g
Percentage of total calories from fat	52%
of which saturates	8%

88 GREEN BEAN, PUMPKIN, AND OKRA STIR-FRY

per portion serving 6

Kilocalories	101
Kilojoules	419
Protein	2g
Carbohydrate	6g
Dietary Fiber	2g

Good source of potassium, iron, thiamin, niacin, folate, vitamin A, C & E.

Fat	8g
of which saturates	2g
of which monounsaturates	3g
of which polyunsaturates	2g
Percentage of total calories from fat	71%
of which saturates	9%

92 SALAD OF VINE FRUITS WITH GINGER, CHILI, AND MINT SYRUP

per portion seving 6

Kilocalories	124
Kilojoules	528
Protein	less than 1
Carbohydrate	32g
Dietary Fiber	1g

Good source of potassium, vitamin C.

Fat	negligible
Percentage of total calories from fat	2%
of which saturates	negligible

92 COMPÔTE OF DARK FRUITS WITH BAY SYRUP

per portion serving 8

Kilocalories	175
Kilojoules	745
Protein	1g
Carbohydrate	42g
Dietary Fiber	2g

Good source of potassium, vitamin C & E.

Fat	1g
of which saturates	neglible
of which monounsaturates	neglible
of which polyunsaturates	neglible
Percentage of total calories from fat	6%
of which saturates	neglible

94 PAPAYA AND PISTACHIO CHOCOLATE TORTE WITH GINGER RICOTTA CREAM

per portion serving 10

Kilocalories	181
Kilojoules	758
Protein	7g
Carbohydrate	21g
Dietary Fiber	1g

Good source of calcium, potassium, iron, zinc, selenium, riboflavin, vitamin B12, folate, A & E.

Fat	8g
of which saturates	3g
of which monounsaturates	3g
of which polyunsaturates	1g
Percentage of total calories from fat	41%
of which saturates	14%

96 RICE PUDDING WITH DRIED FRUITS AND POMEGRANATES

per portion serving 6

Kilocalories	272
Kilojoules	1150
Protein	12g
Carbohydrate	33g
Dietary Fiber	2g

Good source of calcium, potassium, iron, zinc, iodine, thiamin, riboflavin, niacin, vitamin B6, B12, A & E.

Fat	11g
of which saturates	6g
of which monounsaturates	4g
of which polyunsaturates	1g
Percentage of total calories from fat	37%
of which saturates	18%

96 MANGO AND BLOOD ORANGE WHIP

per portion serving 4

Kilocalories	159
Kilojoules	679
Protein	4g
Carbohydrate	37g
Dietary Fiber	5g

Good source of calcium, potassium, iron, iodine, thiamin, riboflavin, niacin, vitamin B6, folate, A, C & E.

Fat	less than 1g
of which saturates	less than 1g
of which monounsaturates	less than 1g
of which polyunsaturates	less than 1g
Percentage of total calories from fat	4%
of which saturates	1%

98 PEAR AND BERRY PURÉE WITH ROSEMARY SHORTBREAD

per portion serving 4

Kilocalories	505
Kilojoules	2126
Protein	6g
Carbohydrate	88g
Dietary Fiber	7g

Good source of calcium, potassium, iron, iodine, thiamin, niacin, vitamin B6, B12, folate, A, C & E.

Fat	14g
of which saturates	8g
of which monounsaturates	3g
of which polyunsaturates	1g
Percentage of total calories from fat	24%
of which saturates	14%

102 PAPAYA AND PINEAPPLE JUICE

per portion serving 1

Kilocalories	128
Kilojoules	550
Protein	2g
Carbohydrate	32g
Dietary Fiber	5g

Good source of potassium, thiamin, vitamin B6, folate, A & C.

Fat	less than 1g
of which saturates	less than 1g
of which monounsaturates	less than 1g
of which polyunsaturates	less than 1g
Percentage of total calories from fat	4%
of which saturates	2%

102 APPLE AND GRAPE JUICE

per portion serving 1

Kilocalories	144
Kilojoules	618
Protein	1g
Carbohydrate	37g
Dietary Fiber	4g

Good source of potassium, thiamin, vitamin B6, folate, C & E.

Fat	less than 1g
of which saturates	less than 1g
of which monounsaturates	less than 1g
of which polyunsaturates	less than 1g
Percentage of total calories from fat	2%
of which saturates	1%

102 CELERY AND LETTUCE JUICE

per portion serving 1

Kilocalories	47
Kilojoules	205
Protein	2g
Carbohydrate	6g
Dietary Fiber	5g

Good source of potassium, iron, thiamin, niacin, vitamin B6, folate, A, C & E.

Fat	2g
of which saturates	less than 1g
of which monounsaturates	0g
of which polyunsaturates	less than 1g
Percentage of total calories from fat	30%
of which saturates	4%

104 SWEET DREAM SWEETMEATS

per portion serving 16

Kilocalories	44
Kilojoules	187
Protein	1g
Carbohydrate	9g
Dietary Fiber	1g

Good source of potassium, iron, niacin, vitamin B6 and E.

Fat	1g
of which saturates	less than 1g
of which monounsaturates	less than 1g
of which polyunsaturates	less than 1g
Percentage of total calories from fat	18%
of which saturates	2%

104 APRICOT, BANANA, AND ELDERFLOWER GELATIN DESSERT

per portion serving 2

Kilocalories	141
Kilojoules	604
Protein	2g
Carbohydrate	34g
Dietary Fiber	5g

Good source of potassium, iron, niacin, and folate.

Fat	less than 1g
of which saturates	less than 1g
of which monounsaturates	less than 1g
of which polyunsaturates	less than 1g
Percentage of total calories from fat	3%
of which saturates	less than 1%

106 HOT NUTMEG AND GINGER MILK

per portion serving 1

Kilocalories	104
Kilojoules	443
Protein	8g
Carbohydrate	11g
Dietary Fiber	0

Good source of calcium, potassium, iodine, riboflavin, vitamin B12, and folate.

Fat	4g
of which saturates	3g
of which monounsaturates	1g
of which polyunsaturates	0
Percentage of total calories from fat	34%
of which saturates	22%

106 LIME FLOWER TEA

per portion serving 1

Kilocalories	2
Kilojoules	25
Protein	0
Carbohydrate	less than 1g
Dietary Fiber	0
Fat	0
of which saturates	0
of which monounsaturates	0
of which polyunsaturates	0
Percentage of total calories from fat	0
of which saturates	0

106 HOT CIDER VINEGAR AND HONEY

per portion serving 1

Kilocalories	19
Kilojoules	83
Protein	less than 1g
Carbohydrate	5g
Dietary Fiber	0
Fat	0
of which saturates	0
of which monounsaturates	0
of which polyunsaturates	0
Percentage of total calories from fat	0
of which saturates	0

Mail-Order Food Sources

GENERAL

ARKANSAS
Mountain Ark Trading Company,
120 S East Street
Fayetteville, AR 72701.
Tel (501) 442-7191.
Organic and traditional Oriental foods.

CALIFORNIA
Adams Ranch Gourmet Olives and Olive Oil,
Bob Bente, P O Box 821, Meadow
Vista, CA 95722.
Tel (916) 878-2143.

The Chinese Grocer,
209 Post St at Grant Ave, San
Francisco, CA 94108.
Tel (415) 982-0125 or 800-227-3320

Frank's Fresh Foods, Inc,
461 Crystal Springs Road, St Helena,
CA 94574.
Tel (707) 963-8354.
Smoked fowl, meat, fish, and seafood.

Gold Mine Natural Foods,
1947 30th Street, San Diego,
CA, 92102.
Tel 800-475-3663.

Gourmet Mushrooms, Inc,
P O Box 391, Sebastopol CA 95473.
Tel (707) 823-1743.

Jaffe brothers,
P O Box 636, Valley Center,
CA 92082-0636.
Tel (619) 749-1133.

Lundberg Family Farms,
P O Box 369, Richvale, CA 95974.
Tel (916) 882-4551.
Brown rice and blends of rice types.

Malibu Greens,
P O Box 6286, Malibu, CA 90264.
Tel 1-800-383-1414.

Ocean Harvest Sea Vegetables,
P O Box 1719, Mendocino, CA 95460.
Tel (707) 964-7869.

G B Ratto, International Grocers,
821 Washington St, Oakland,
CA 94607.
Tel 1-800-228-3515 in California;
1-800-325-3483 outside California.

Timber Crest Farms,
4791 Dry Creek Road, Healdsburg,
CA 95448.
Tel (707) 433-8251.

Westbrae Natural Foods,
Attn: Ms Lynne Minsky,
1065 East Walut Street, Carson,
CA 90746.
Tel (310) 886-8200.

FLORIDA
Earl Ebersol Farms,
27828 S W 127th Avenue,
Homestead, FL 33032.
Tel (305) 247-3905.

Health Centre for Better Living,
6189 Taylor Rd, Naples, FL 33942.

Lakewood Natural Products,
P O Box 420708, Miami, FL 33242.
Tel (305) 324-5932.

Tree of Life,
Attn: Dot Peck,
P O Box 410, St Augustine, FL 32085.
Tel (904) 825-2042.

HAWAII
Shojin/Golden Sun,
P O Box 247, Kealakekua, HI 96750.
Tel (808) 322-3651.

ILLINOIS
Geo Cornille & Sons Produce,
60 South Water Market, Chicago,
Illinois 60608.
Tel (312) 226-1015.

Star Market,
3349 North Clark Street, Chicago,
Illinois 60657.
Tel (312) 472-0599.
Asian dry goods and produce.

MAINE
Maine Coast Sea Vegetables,
Shore Road, Franklin, ME 04634.
Tel (207) 565-2907.

MARYLAND
Organic Foods Express,
11003 Emack Road, Beltsville, MD
20705.
Tel (301) 816-4944.

MASSACHUSSETS
South River Miso Company, Inc,
South River Farm, Conway,
MA 01341.

US Mills, Inc,
Attn: Mr. Charles Verde,
395 Elliot Street, Newton Upper
Falls, MA 02164.
Tel (617) 969-5400.

MICHIGAN
American Spoon Foods,
P O Box 566, Petoskey, MI 49770.
Tel (800) 222-5886.

Eden Foods, Inc,
701 Tecumseh Road, Clinton,
MI 49236.
Tel (517) 456-7424.

NEW JERSEY
Edward and Sons Trading Co,
P O Box 3150, 1091 Lousons Road,
Union, NJ 07083.
Tel (201) 964-8176.

NEW YORK
Dean & DeLuca Retail and Mail-Order Department,
560 Broadway, New York, NY 10012.
Tel (212) 431-1691.

East West Products, Ltd,
P O Box 1210, New York, NY 10025.
Tel (212) 864-5508 or 800-542-6544.

NEW MEXICO
Chili Shop,
109 East Water Street, Santa Fe,
NM 87501.
Tel (505) 983-6080.

Los Chileros de Nuevo Mexico,
P O Box 6215, Santa Fe, NM 87502.
Tel (505) 471-6967.

NORTH CAROLINA
Great Eastern Sun, Attn: Mr. Don
DeBona, 92 McIntosh Road,
Asheville, NC 28806.
Tel (704) 252-3090.

Macrobiotic Wholesale Company,
Attn: Kurt and Else Schmitz,
799 Old Leicester Highway,
Asheville, NC 28806,
Tel. (704) 252-1221.

PENNSYLVANIA
Great Valley Mills,
687 Mill Rd, Telford, PA 18969.

Walnut Acres,
Penns Creek, PA 17862.
Tel (717) 847-0601
or 1-800-433-3993.
Flours, cereals, grains. Catalog available.

TEXAS
Arrowhead Mills, Inc,
P O Box 2059, Hereford, TX 79045.
Tel (806) 364-0730.

Texas Wild Game Cooperative,
P O Box 530, Ingram,
TX 78025. Tel (800) 962-4263.

VERMONT
The Cook's Garden,
P O Box 535, Londonderry, VT 05148.
Tel (802) 824-3400.

The Herb Closet,
104 Main Street, Montpelier,
VT 05602.
Tel (802) 223-0888.
Full line of Ayurvedic herbs and formulas.

WASHINGTON
Cascadian Farms,
311 Dillard Street, Concrete,
WA 98237.
Tel. (206) 853-8175.

Flora, Inc,
P O Box 950, 805 E Badger Rd,
Lynden, WA 98264.
Tel (206) 354-2110 or 800-446-2110.
Oils pressed without heat, air, or light.

The Herb Farm,
32804 Issaquah-Fall City Rd, Fall
City, WA 98024.
Tel 1-800-866-HERB.

Granum, Inc,
Attn: Mr. Blake
Rankin, 2901 N E Blakeley Street,
Seattle, WA 98105.
Tel (206) 525-0051.

INDIAN FOODS AND SPICES
India Groceries and Spices,
10633 West North Ave, Wauwatosa,
WI 53226.
Tel (414) 771-3535.

India Sweets and Spices,
9409 Venice Boulevard, Los Angeles,
CA 90230.
Tel (310) 837-5286.

Indian Grocery Store,
2342 Douglas Road, Coral Gables,
FL 33134.
Tel (305) 448-5869.

Seema Enterprises,
10616 Page Avenue, St Louis,
MO 63132.
Tel (314) 423-9990.

Annapurna,
127 East 28th Street, New York,
NY 10016.
Tel (212) 889-7540.

Foods of India,
Sinha Trading Company,
120 Lexington Avenue, New York,
NY 10016.
Tel (212) 683-4419.

House of Spices,
4101 Walnut Street, Philadelphia,
PA 19104.
Tel (215) 222-1111.

FRESH HERBS
Sandy Mush Herb Nursery,
316 Surrett Cove Road, Leicester, NC
28748-9622.
Tel (704) 683-2014.
Catalog: $4

Logee's Greenhouses,
141 North Street, Danielson,
CN 06239.
Catalog: $3.

Tinmouth Channel Farm,
Box 428B-HCD, Tinmouth,
VT 05773.
Catalog: $2.

Brown's Edgewood Gardens,
2611 Corrine Drive, Orlando,
FL 32803.
Tel (407) 896-3203.
Catalog: $2.

Vineyard Sound Herbs,
RFD 900, Vineyard Haven, MA 02568.
Tel (508) 696-7574.
Catalog: $1.

Lily of the Valley Herb Farm,
3969 Fox Avenue, Minerva,
OH 44657.
Tel (216) 862-3920.
Plant & seed list: $1; product list: $1.

HEALTH ASSOCIATIONS

American Herbalists Guild
P O Box 1683,
Soquel, CA 95073

American Holistic Health Association
P O Box 17400,
Anaheim, CA 90017-7100
Tel (714) 779-6152/777-2917.

American Institute of Homeopathy
1585 Glencoe Street, Suite 44,
Denver, CO 80220-1338.
Tel (303) 321-4105.

American Dietetics Association
216 West Jackson Boulevard
Apt 800, Chicago, IL 60606-6995
Tel (800) 877-1600

American Association of Ayurvedic Medicine
P.O. Box 598,
South Lancaster, MA 01561,
Tel 800-843-8332.
Fax (201) 777-1197.

International Association of Holistic Health Practitioners
5020 West Spring Mountain Road,
Las Vegas, NV 89102.
Tel (702) 873-4542.

American Association of Nutrition Consultants
1641 East Sunset Road
Apt B-117, Las Vegas, NV 89119
Tel. (709) 361-1132

American Naturopathic Medical Association
P O Box 19221,
Las Vegas, NV 89132.
Tel (702) 796-9067.

American Association for Acupuncture and Oriental Medicine
4101 Lake Boone Trail,
Suite 201,
Raleigh, NC 27607.
Tel (919) 787 5181.

American Holistic Association
4101 Lake Boone Trail,
Suite 201,
Raleigh, NC 27607.
Tel (919) 787-5181.
Fax (919) 787-4916.

American Association of Oriental Medicine (AAOM)
433 Front Street,
Catasauqua, PA 18032.
Tel (610) 266 1433.
Fax (610) 264-2768.

Association of Holistic Healing Centers
109 Holly Crescent,
Suite 201,
Virginia Beach, VA 23451.
Tel (804) 422-9033.
Fax (804) 422-8132.

American Association of Naturopathic Physicians
P O Box. 20386,
Seattle, WA 98102.
Tel (206) 323-7610.

National Acupuncture and Oriental Medicine Alliance (National Alliance)
14637 Starr Road SE,
Olalla, WA 98359.
Tel (206) 851 6896.
Fax (206) 851 6883.

National Acupuncture and Oriental Medicine Alliance
P.O. Box 77511,
Seattle, WA 98177-0531.
Tel (206) 524-3511.

Index